Gathe[

Deborah Steward

Written by Deborah Steward.

Designed by Mark Jessett & Kevin Steward
Food Stylist: Grace Steward
Illustrations: Mark Jessett

Photography:
Deborah and Kevin Steward, their family and staff
Peter Smith of Newbery Smith Photography
Cover photograph by Shannon Warby

All the recipes in this book have been tried and tested by
Deborah Steward and her family but no responsibility can be
taken for their outcome as ovens, ingredients
and cooking techniques can differ.

Every effort has been made to trace copyright holders
and to obtain their permission for the use of copyright material.
The publisher apologises for any errors or omissions
in the above list and would be grateful if notified of any
corrections that should be incorporated in future reprints
or editions of this book.

All information is believed to be correct at the time of publication,
and whilst every effort has been made to provide accurate
up-to-date information, readers aware of any errors
or omissions can contact the publisher.

The author has asserted her moral rights.
Copyright © 2020 Deborah Steward
www.deborahsteward.co.uk
All rights reserved
This edition August 2020

For Mum and Dad with my love

Contents

5.	Introduction
8.	The start of things to come
11.	The Queen's Golden Jubilee
16.	Amazing Grace
21.	My other half
26.	Into and out of the darkness
32.	A grand send-off
36.	Forces of Nature
41.	A wet and windy day out in North Norfolk
45.	A day at the races
50.	Wild life
54.	All cookers great and small
61.	Boys will be boys
65.	Three wheels on our wagon
68.	Lamb in the van
72.	Dogs, dicks and doorknobs
76.	Oh, we do like to be beside the seaside!
80.	Mermaid's Brazilian carnival ball
86.	Whoops-a-daisy
91.	Wild, wild West Norfolk
96.	Our American road trip
104.	Our American road trip. Part 2
110.	Recipes

Quince jellly, Quince membrillo, Pavlova, Duck with damsons and oranges
Luscious lemon cake, Roast carrot and fennel soup, Grace's amazing cheese scones
Country terrine, Treacle tart, Roast beef and Yorkshire puddings, Raspberry dumplings
Vegetable pakoras, Queen of puddings Spotted dick, Apple and date chutney
Kev's perfect bacon sandwich, Nanny's lavender shortbread, Brazilian roast pork
Smoked trout pâté, Kev's fried chicken, Molten chocolate puddings
Dan's ham and bean soup, Debs chicken wiggle.

135.	Your home recipes and notes
176.	Conversion table 1
177.	Conversion table 2
178.	About the author

Introduction

Where do I start? It would be fair to say that I come from a family of people who are unusually interested in food. From a very early age I can remember pheasants hanging on the back of the shed door when they were in season, waiting to be plucked by Mum when she could fit it in around caring for her large and loud family! Dad would almost always have something ready to harvest from either our garden or his allotment - crisp green callaloo from his native Jamaica, or perfectly sweet carrots complete with clumps of wet soil.

Various uncles, aunts, brothers, sisters, nephews and nieces would often appear with bags of delicious, freshly gathered food too... wonderful walnuts, baskets of wild mushrooms (although we never found out the closely guarded secret of where they came from), half a dozen freshly caught mackerel that were almost too beautiful to eat, a handful of ruby red autumn raspberries... the list goes on and on. Maybe that is where my love of food began, being close to such bountiful, premium, seasonal ingredients, collected by family and prepared with care. Nowadays those words are used with abandon on restaurant menus the length and breadth of this land, but when I was growing up it was a given that what you ate was good, nourishing fare which was prepared with love.

In my life as a chef I have strived to carry this idea and my love of beautiful produce forward, making full use of the rhythm of the seasons, and carefully preparing the very best ingredients to show

Introduction

them off and do them proud. I think my very favourite and busiest time of the year is harvest time, when there is so much produce and so little time to prepare it all. It is a big challenge to pick, prepare and bottle chutney, jam and pickle while the ingredients are both plentiful and either cheap or free, but the end results are glorious! There is something lovely about squirrelling away food at a time of plenty to be able to enjoy it later on when the season has passed, and the further enjoyment is remembering who you picked it with and the fun you had doing it.

The tradition of bartering is alive and well in this part of Norfolk, and long may it continue! Often we get a phone call to say 'Deb, the quinces and medlars are ready' sometime in late October, and we then head off to carefully pick them. This can be a hazardous job as anyone who has done it will appreciate and we should really wear crash helmets, but we turn our harvest into the most fabulous crystal-clear jelly and dark, sticky membrillo to have alongside cheese at Christmas time. In return for this generosity, a few days before Christmas, a basket of preserves will find its way back to where it came from, to be enjoyed over the festive period... deal done!

Introduction

The start of things to come

When my girls were very small I had kept my hand in catering, so to speak, by making the odd wedding or birthday cake. One day, I got a call asking if I would be able to do a wedding cake for someone in our village. It all seemed fairly straightforward, as the idea was that they would be doing the food for the whole event themselves and I would just be responsible for the cake. As the weeks went by, I kept receiving phone calls from the bride-to-be, who knew that I used to cook professionally, asking if it would be possible for me to make some meringues for them and perhaps a few salads etc, etc…

As the date drew nearer, these calls became increasingly frequent. One morning, just five days before the big day, I answered the phone to hear the bride-to-be in a complete flat-out panic. It transpired that amidst all the wedding plans no one had given any thought whatsoever as to who would be serving the guests, nor what they would be eating and drinking from! Did I know anyone who may be able to help serve food? Did I know where to hire linen from? Did I know anyone who may be able to serve drinks?

Well, I have to tell you, I felt so sorry that someone who should be looking forward to her big day was in such a muddle that I told her I would do my level best to help as much as I could. The next day I was on the phone for the best part of the morning, doing my best to contact people I used to work with in the hotel trade, friends and family, in fact anyone who I thought may be able to assist. My contacts came up

The start of things to come

trumps and I was able to call the bride-to-be back a few hours later and tell her that I had a linen and china supplier, drinks staff, waiting staff and chefs, all lined up and good to go. The big day dawned and the reality of the task we had set ourselves was almost overwhelming. To say it was a baptism of fire was an understatement... Thankfully the whole day went like clockwork, from the laying of the tables in the morning, to serving the last pint of beer 15 hours later. Needless to say we did not have any trouble sleeping that night; we were all completely exhausted, both physically and mentally. Over the next few days, after the dust had settled, we realised how very much we had all enjoyed the whole experience. Kev, my husband, and I discussed at length whether there was a possibility that we could find a way to eventually build up a small business catering for events in our part of Norfolk.

At this point I should say that I had quite a lot of experience in catering and cooking for large numbers of people, as my early career had involved working as a chef in hotels and restaurants. I had given all that up to concentrate on raising our two little girls, but I now felt that the time was right to test the waters to see if it would be possible to try working for myself as it was such a long-held ambition. As time went on, word got around that we had successfully organised the catering for the wedding and I started to get a few calls asking if I would be able to cook for the odd dinner party, drinks party or small reception. With help from the original team we were able to do a few of these and really that's how the outside catering business took off. That original wedding cake request, as it turned out, would change our lives forever.

The start of things to come

The Queen's Golden Jubilee

2002 was the year Her Majesty the Queen celebrated 50 years on the throne, and as part of the celebrations it was decided to hold a large garden party reception in the grounds of Sandringham House. A year earlier, one morning in 2001, we got a phone call asking if we would be interested in being part of the team who would be supplying the catering for this prestigious event.

Of course we were thrilled at being asked and agreed straight away. In due course we had a meeting with the other members of the team, which comprised other Norfolk caterers and chefs, all of whom, except one, were ladies. There were ten separate teams in total, as well as catering students from the King's Lynn, Norwich and Yarmouth colleges who had been asked to serve the food that we prepared. It was certainly a great opportunity for us all and we were honoured to be included. We were to provide canapés for 4,000 people in total, which is an awful lot of food, so it was decided the easiest way to do it would be to break it down into a much more manageable 400 people per team.

Preparations for such a large event started about a year in advance, so that everyone involved would get to know one another and be able to work together as a team on the day. The plan was that each separate team would prepare six of their favourite canapés, making 60 in total. We would then all get together and taste them, and then have a vote on the best six that would go on to be served on the big day. The day

The Queen's Golden Jubilee

of the tasting arrived and one of my six canapés had, as the principal ingredient, some delicious hot-smoked trout that my Dad catches and then smokes himself back at the commercial kitchen where we are based. This delicious fish would form the filling in a delicate and very pretty mini spinach roulade. We all enjoyed the process of seeing what each of us had prepared and the blind tasting that followed in order to help choose the favourite six. As luck would have it, they chose my roulade to be one of them. The next question was, would my Dad and all his friends at the fishing club of which he is a member, be able to supply the 9 kg of fish required to fill enough roulade for four thousand people? After a quick ring round, we knew it would be possible, so we were all set to roll. All we had to do was wait for the day of the party to draw near, so we were, by this point, all very excited and nervous at the same time.

The next few months were for us exceptionally busy and time flew by quickly. Before we knew it, it was less than a week until the big day. Five days before the event I had a phone call from the lady who was organising the party, saying she had something she wanted to ask me. She wanted to know if we would agree to be part of a television programme the BBC was producing about the Golden Jubilee celebrations. She had spoken to the BBC team and had happened to mention the local trout that my Dad was going to supply, and someone thought it would be an interesting piece to have in the programme. The plan was, if we agreed, to film Dad fishing at the lake, bringing the fish back to our kitchen and hot-smoking them, and then I would do a demonstration of the roulade that I would be making for the party. On the day itself they would also like to film us arriving at Sandringham, setting up and preparing the food. Well, I have to say I hesitated for all of ten seconds before I said yes, of course, we would be delighted!

When I put the phone down the reality of what I had just agreed to set in. Not only were we undertaking the most high-profile event we had ever worked on, but I had just agreed to have a film crew shadowing us beforehand and on the day itself... no pressure then! Later on that night, tossing and turning in bed, I wondered if I had actually taken

The Queen's Golden Jubilee

leave of my senses. Two days later, the film crew arrived at the lake to meet my Dad and film the fishing sequence. All went well except for the fact that the trout were not having any of it. Do you think he could get a bite? It was all a bit embarrassing, so Dad asked a few fellow anglers if they would join him in the hunt for the elusive fish. They wished one another 'tight lines' and set off with steely determination. Before long it was clear that there would be no fish landed that morning.

Luckily, Dad had a bit of insurance up his sleeve... he had brought one he had prepared earlier! He had gone to the lake the day before and caught a beauty, anticipating the worst-case scenario that if he couldn't get a bite when they were filming, at least he had a fish he could put on the line and pretend to reel in, which is exactly what he did! Mission accomplished, the crew then came to our kitchen to film Dad as he smoked the fish. I then did my piece to camera and filled and rolled the roulade. After all the excitement we all sat down together for lunch, and it was a great atmosphere. The next couple of days passed in a blur as we had a lot of preparation to do and not much time left to do it in, but I am glad to say we were ready in good time and were looking forward to what the next day would bring.

We awoke early the next morning to the most glorious day imaginable, with sunshine and brilliant, clear blue skies. We set off to the kitchen to load up with every single item that we might need for the job in hand. We had quite a long list of things that had to be ticked off and put in the van, as we knew we absolutely could not forget a single thing. Kev, Jo and myself jumped into the van and off we went. We arrived at Sandringham exactly on time to find the film crew already there ready to film our arrival. As they did so, we proceeded to get ourselves organised. We were going to be working out of two enormous marquees that had each been equipped with five identical kitchen areas, each with tables, refrigeration and running water. It is a huge logistical challenge to organise an event of this size, but we had everything we needed and we were able to start the food preparations on schedule. It did seem strange working in such close proximity to people who in different circumstances would be considered rivals, but

The Queen's Golden Jubilee

everyone was so pleased to be there it just didn't seem to matter at all. It was a great atmosphere and the next few hours flew by, so much so that before we knew it, it was game on.

The students and their tutors had all arrived and, to my delight, my very favourite tutor from my time at King's Lynn College was accompanying the students from there and we were to work together during service. As far as I was concerned, the day was just getting better and better. The two-and-a-half hours went like clockwork and we all managed to synchronise the canapés so that we were all serving the same course at the same time. Although we were being filmed on and off at the time we didn't really take a lot of notice as we were all so focused on the job in hand. It was all over before we knew it: the last bite had been eaten, the last glass of wine had been sipped and it was time to pack everything away and go home.

The sun was beginning to go down and there was a lovely soft golden light by now. As we drove away we glanced back over to the marquee. We felt tired and a little bit sad that it was all over, but at the same time incredibly proud of being part of such a momentous day. We had set our video to record the whole BBC programme as it had been broadcast live, so when we got home we watched it and were thrilled at the whole thing - especially Dad landing THAT trout. Poor thing, it didn't seem to have a lot of fight left in it!

The Queen's Golden Jubilee

Amazing Grace

Holkham Country Fair is one of the highlights of the summer for a huge number of people in Norfolk. Set against the backdrop of the magnificent Holkham Hall, it is a traditional country fair celebrating all things outdoor, from crafts, dog handling and fishing, to all kinds of country activities. It really is a great weekend for young and old alike. For us it means we provide the catering for the Vice Presidents' enclosure, and we also look after the food requirements for whichever military band has been requested to play that year.

In effect, we set up a pop-up restaurant, as well as a tea room and field kitchen, complete with gas ranges, refrigeration and everything we need to cook, store and prepare to feed upwards of 500 people over the weekend... all in a huge marquee in the middle of the parkland. As you can imagine, the whole event takes a lot of careful thought and planning. With every outside event, no matter how much you plan and look at the long-range weather forecasts, you can never be sure what will happen on the day. One particular year we duly arrived on the Friday to set up and prepare for a supper party that was being held in the tea room section of the marquee on the eve of the fair in order to raise funds for the Army Benevolent Fund.

Most of that day it had been raining on and off, alternating with sunshine and a little bit of a breeze. Unfortunately, just before we were due to leave, the heavens opened. Last-minute phone calls were made to ask the staff to bring wellies or waterproof shoes as things were not looking good. It then proceeded to pour down in a way you don't expect to see in the middle of July. Nevertheless, we just had to carry on regardless. The highlight of the evening was to be a Beating Retreat, performed by that year's band - the Royal Minden (now part of The Band of The Queen's Division) - in the main arena but, by the time they were due to appear, we had a flood in the catering area and so had to lay down wooden pallets to stand on whilst serving the buffet supper. Not a good start, considering it was only Friday and we still had Saturday and Sunday to go!

Of course a little thing like a downpour was not going to stop the Royal Minden Band. Being the true professionals that they are, out they went and performed their whole programme as if it was a balmy summer evening. After the Retreat the band came in and played a few numbers in the marquee to finish off the evening's entertainment and they then left to rousing applause. We duly served supper for 100 Army Benevolent Fund guests and around 50 band members, cleared up, battened down the openings in the marquee, and went home. I think we all said a silent prayer for better weather the next day.

The next morning, as we had feared, was more of the same at the start of the day, but it did clear up later so we were able to get on well with the preparations for lunch without too much inconvenience. The day went well and we were all pleased with the way things had gone; occasionally the sun managed to break through and when that happened it was a lovely place to be. In spite of the weather, the crowds were still arriving and enjoying the lovely surroundings.

Sunday dawned, but oh dear! We had largely got away with it on Saturday, but the next day the rain was back with a vengeance, the sky was dark and we knew we were in for a long, long day. The band still went out in the pouring rain to do their morning routine although, as you can imagine, the audience numbers were well down. Just as they came back in to their side of the marquee, Grace, our youngest daughter, was in the process of removing some cheese scones from the oven. She had made a big batch for the staff as a bit of a mid-morning morale booster because we were all starting to flag. As I am sure you would agree, there is nothing quite like the smell of freshly baked cheese scones when you are cold, wet, hungry and wishing you were somewhere else!

The band trudged in, absolutely drenched through, and looked longingly at the cooling scones, Grace caught their looks and glanced across at me. I knew exactly what she was thinking, (mother and daughter telepathy is a marvellous thing), so I nodded to her and she proceeded to take the entire batch through to the band's side of the marquee. To say they fell on them with abandon was the understatement of the year! In less than five minutes all that was left were a few crumbs, so Grace quickly made another batch for us and, believe me, they disappeared just as quickly.

By now we were almost at lunchtime and so we cracked on and managed to get it all served without too much drama. After lunch came the big clear-up; everything had to be cleaned down, packed away and loaded into the waiting vans - always the worst part of the job and, funnily enough... it was still raining. By this point, staff morale was understandably low. We were tired, cold and longing to call it a day, but as they say, every cloud has a silver lining... Fifteen minutes before the band was due to go out to play its last set, the Regimental Sergeant Major marched up to me and asked where Grace could be found. She was sitting at the far end of the kitchen counting napkins and putting them into laundry bags. Without another word, all 50 members of the Royal Minden Band formed a circle around her (and the napkins) and proceeded to play 'Amazing Grace' for our daughter of the same name!

It was one of those moments that all who were present will never forget. It is the most moving hymn at the best of times, but in the final hours of a pretty stressful weekend I have to say more than a few of us wiped a tear or two away. Sarah, one of the organisers of the show, was in the restaurant at the time and came through to listen, as did some of the diners.

It was very special. When they had finished playing, Grace looked up and said, 'Well, you don't get that every day!' and we all fell about laughing. The band turned around and marched out into the pouring rain for one last time. All in all, it was quite a weekend!

Amazing Grace

20

My other half

My husband Kev and I have been together since we met at high school at the tender age of 16, so we really grew up together... and stayed together! We were married in 1985, and are blessed with two very special daughters, Amii-Rose and Grace. Kev started his working life in agricultural engineering, and then moved into car sales for a number of local garages. We had just started to build our catering business and were both working long hours at weekends and evenings as it's the very nature of what we do that we work when other people are off. It goes with the territory, so to speak.

It soon became obvious that Kev could not carry on working such long hours in catering on top of holding down a full-time job. We had always said that if we were not working for ourselves by the time we were 40 years old, it probably was not going to happen - so it was decision time. We had our two little girls so we had to think long and hard about what we were doing, as we had a lot at stake if things didn't work out as planned. After lots of careful thought and consideration, on the eve of his 39th birthday Kev finished work at the garage and we embarked on the most amazing career together.

We were lucky in that we had several large events booked that first summer, so we jumped straight into it, happily immersing ourselves in the job, and we pretty soon realised that we had made the right choice, both for our family and our work. Kev - as I always call him, has the most amazing ability to keep calm and collected in any given situation, which is a tremendous gift to have, especially in our line of work. I, on the other hand, can be inclined to go off half-cocked and don't always think practically, so between us we are good as a whole!

When Kev was a little boy he was rather indulged: he used to get the latest and most expensive toys bought for him at birthdays and Christmas. After a while playing with them conventionally he would inevitably take them apart to see how they worked. This curiosity has stood him in good stead as it allowed him to develop a great understanding of how mechanical things work, as well as all things electrical. Over the years this ability has helped us out of many a predicament, not to mention saved us a small fortune in repair bills!

When we are out on site working in a marquee for instance, the people who put up the marquee do their job and then leave. The electrician will then do his job, after which he will leave too. Later on, if a problem develops we are the only ones on site, so it will invariably fall on Kev's shoulders to sort it out so we can carry on with our job. If we are to be barbecuing say, and we have a sudden downpour, Kev will appear with a tarpaulin and a handful of trusty cable ties and voilà... no more soggy chefs! Kev has become known as our very own Ray Mears: if you were stranded on a desert island, he would be the one to light the fire and provide shelter from the elements, whereas I, on the other hand, may be able to rustle up dinner!

During our working life together he has done some truly extraordinary things, mostly involving helping someone out of a predicament. Once he literally gave the shirt off his back to the father of a young lady whose 21st birthday party we were catering for. It was awful weather that night, absolutely bucketing down. On his way to the party, the girl's dad had jumped out of his car to put up a sign showing guests the way to the venue. As he was hammering the sign into the ground, he slipped and fell into a field that was full of sheep... and sheep muck! The poor man came back to the venue absolutely filthy. As the dress code was 'white tie' he had on a black tailcoat and was now wearing a waistcoat, shirt and tie that were all a rather fetching shade of green!

My other half

After fighting the urge to burst out laughing, Kev, bless him, took off his own white shirt, black waistcoat and tie, and gave them to him so he could greet the guests. Fortunately ever-resourceful Kev had some spare clothes in the van that he could use himself.

Another time we were at a party at which a young man had been enthusiastically dancing all night, so much so that the sole of his shoe completely fell off! He happened to be a size 11 and, luckily for him, so is Kev, who once more came to the rescue with a spare pair of shoes so that the young man was able to continue grooving until the early hours. Kev thought he probably would never see his shoes again, so was rather pleasantly surprised when we arrived the next morning to clear the marquee down and there by the back door stood his shoes, polished to a high shine and accompanied by a letter of grateful thanks.

By now you may have noticed a trend that there is no telling what essential item of equipment or clothing is to be found in one of Kev's vans. Once he had an old Toyota that was christened the 'Mystery Machine' as it really was a mystery how much stuff would go in and also appear from its cavernous interior. Certainly only Kev knew exactly what was in there and where to find it. Once we were at a wedding in an old barn when, lo and behold, just before the guests arrived, a mole decided to come scurrying through the kitchen area. Completely unfazed Kev went to the Mystery Machine and appeared, accompanied by hoots of laughter from the staff, with what he described as his mole catcher's gauntlets! In fact he had been shopping a couple of days before and had bought a couple of pairs of cheap gardening gloves that he had not got round to taking out of the van. It was priceless!

Another time we had been asked to provide a traditional afternoon tea to celebrate the wedding of a local couple. The event was to be held in a marquee beside the tiny village church where the wedding was to take place, not far from where we live. As they started to leave the church and walk to the marquee, we soon realised that there were far more guests in attendance than we had been asked to cater for.

My other half

Kev quickly found the bride's Mum and asked her to confirm how many guests were now expecting to be fed. She told him, somewhat sheepishly, that she had in fact lost count as when she had run out of invitation cards, she had just carried on asking the rest of the guests verbally. She had no idea how many people had said yes - it could be anything between 100 and 150! Kev realised this could be embarrassing for both her and us, so quickly sent someone back to the kitchen to get more food supplies. Then, when he realised there would not be enough seating, he took two waiters with him and proceeded to take the pews out of the church! Kev, and only Kev, would be able to think so quickly on his feet to rescue the situation.

Suffice to say he is ingenious in his ability to somehow find a way around the huge variety of problems that can arise, more often than not when they are least expected. He gets the greatest pleasure in helping someone out of a muddle, and if he is able to do so, he will. He is the kindest, most patient person I know, and certainly the very best thing I have ever done in my life is marry him.

My other half

Into and out of the darkness

During the course of every year we are asked to look after the food requirements for a huge variety of events. It may be a very smart dinner to celebrate a milestone birthday, a high-profile charity fundraiser, or a sumptuous wedding breakfast in a stately home. This huge variety is the most enjoyable aspect of our work, because we never know where we will be asked to go and what we will be asked to do next. One morning I took a phone call asking if we would be able to provide dinner for 20 people one Sunday evening in early winter, followed by a shoot lunch the next day. It was to be held in a rather large house a few miles from where we live.

I asked all the usual questions about what equipment was already there, so I would know what we had to bring by way of china, linen and glassware, as well as how many staff would be required, the timings etc. I did not feel I would need to go over beforehand because although it was a new venue for us, everything seemed pretty straightforward. In due course I submitted some menu suggestions to the lady of the house, from which she chose what she wanted us to prepare.

So far, so good... I was only asked to bring one person to help me in the kitchen as two ladies who worked in the house had been asked to help serve in the dining room, so at about 6 pm on the Sunday evening Tracy and I loaded everything into one of our vans and headed off, even though we would much rather have been sitting at home beside the fire.

Into and out of the darkness

It was a really cold, wet, windy evening and already dark when we arrived. We carefully followed the directions we had been given and went down a long, tree-lined drive. As we approached the house all we could see was the outline of the roof, eerily lit by the wintry moon. The huge Gothic pile looked like it was crouched down waiting for us. It would be fair to say a little shiver went down our spines as we followed the drive to the rear of the house, where we could unload directly into the back door of the kitchen. As we pulled up, we realised the house was in complete darkness. My first thought was that I had somehow made a mistake with the date of the booking and we were here on the wrong night.

Of course nowadays the first thing I would do is phone the clients or Kev to see if indeed we had done just that, but this was long before any of us had mobile phones. As we were in the depths of the countryside there were not even any phone boxes. I got out of the van, leaving the lights on so that I could see where I was going, tapped on the door's huge brass door knocker and waited. No one came, so I rapped harder. Still no one came so I gave it one last attempt and hammered as hard as I could. Just as I turned away to get back in the van and drive home, I heard a huge bolt slide back on the inside of the door and the lady of the house appeared. She apologised that she had not heard us arrive and went on to explain that they had lost the electricity supply about an hour earlier due to the awful weather. She was unable to make contact with the supply company, but, as this was not an unusual occurrence, she wanted to go ahead with the dinner, particularly as all the guests were staying at the house and had already arrived.

The reason that we had been unable to see any lights on within the house was that they had lit some candles and closed the window shutters to help keep the heat in. She explained that luckily they had an Aga and it was stoked up and raring to go, so we would be able to cook on that. Also, she assured us, they had loads more candles and she thought it would be great fun! Now the word 'fun' was not one I would have used, given the situation we were in, but she was adamant that it would be a memorable evening for us all. All the guests were

Into and out of the darkness

ravenously hungry anyway, so whatever we could give them would be greatly appreciated she said, so we agreed to stay and do what we could. The two ladies who were to help serve dinner arrived shortly after and we were shown to a cupboard in the laundry room that was indeed full of candles and torches. The two ladies also assured us this was not an unusual occurrence and off they went to serve drinks and illuminate the dining room, drawing room and hall with a varied assortment of new and used candles. We picked out the biggest candles we could find and proceeded to place them at varying intervals around the enormous kitchen. We also placed a row of ordinary green dinner candles along the back of the Aga so I had some light to cook by.

Tracy had set herself up a little row of nightlights by the sink so she could see to peel the potatoes. Every now and then I would hear her give a nervous laugh, and when I asked her what she was laughing at, she replied that she was reminded of the Elton John song, 'Candle in the wind'. She then proceeded to sing it, cleverly replacing the original words with 'It seemed to me, that she peeled the spuds, by a candle on the sink!' When she had finished with the potatoes, she looked for the bin and couldn't find one anywhere. The two waitresses reappeared and pointed out a small doorway on the wall by the sink: it was a rubbish chute that went straight down into the cellar. It caused us great amusement, as when you dropped something down and waited to the count of three, you could hear the rubbish crash into the bin below.

By this stage in the proceedings I had put the ducks in the oven and was in the middle of making the damson sauce that would accompany them. The puddings were assembled, the vegetables prepared and it was all going surprisingly well, given the situation. The two waitresses were helpful and we all muddled along together. I began to feel that maybe, just maybe, it would all turn out all right. Just before the guests were about to come down, we went through to the dining room. It looked like something out of a film set and was truly spectacular, with the soft glow of candlelight reflecting off the polished glasses on the table. Yet there was something else that was slightly more disturbing:

Into and out of the darkness

peering out at us were the glass eyes of numerous large and small stuffed animals of the furred, feathered or finned varieties, adorning every spare surface and wall space. It was quite spooky as it looked like we were doing a dinner party in the Natural History Museum.

Anyway, back to the kitchen and on with dinner. Tracy and I were just going through the order of things when suddenly someone shouted in a rather cut-glass accent, 'FAK ORF'. We both stood rooted to the spot, thinking we must have misheard when - even louder this time - we heard, 'WILL YOU FAK ORF?' followed by an ear-splitting screech. We were speechless and just stood and stared at each other. Then all hell broke loose. Out of the gloom of the cavernous kitchen, screeching and swearing at the top of its voice, flew the most enormous African Grey parrot. His wingspan must have been one-and-a-half metres (five feet) across and he swooped so low that his feathers touched the top of my hair. Out of sheer fright I screamed out loud and my eyes must have been as big as saucers. He was not happy, not happy at all, and neither was I. Tracy, terrified, fled crying through the back kitchen door and I was not far behind her.

All the time we had been there - getting on for two-and-a-half hours - we were unaware that this foul-mouthed bird had been perched on the end of the curtain pole at the other end of the kitchen. That part of the room was in complete darkness, and he had been watching us, waiting to pick his moment to frighten the living daylights out of us. The two ladies came running in to see what all the commotion was about. As soon as they saw the parrot, Charles, as he happened to be named, they realised what had happened. They were very apologetic, but with all the drama about the power failure they hadn't given a second thought to the fact that he was there and that he might take umbrage at two total strangers invading his space. He was just part of the family as far as they were concerned and they didn't think anything of it as Charles was a free spirit and had the run of the whole house. It seemed he was never ever put in a cage. Just when we thought nothing else could go wrong, I noticed that the candles I had carefully placed on the back of the Aga were by now bending over and leaning in all directions because of the tremendous heat; it looked like a Salvador Dali painting! It would have been hilarious if my sense of humour had, by this stage, not completely deserted me. We only had a few minutes to calm our jangled nerves before it was time to serve dinner. I have to say it all went swimmingly, considering the circumstances. The hosts and guests were full of praise for the dinner we had served them; little did they know how close they came to not getting any dinner at all for a varied assortment of reasons!

Almost all the way home Tracy and I sat in complete silence as the wind and rain buffeted the van. I think we were trying to kid ourselves that what had just happened couldn't possibly really have happened, and each of us was wondering where to start when our other halves asked us how our evening had gone. They say that truth is stranger than fiction and, after an evening like that, that sentiment is one with which I would wholeheartedly agree!

Into and out of the darkness

A grand send-off

Winter can be a harsh along the North Norfolk coast; it can also be incredibly beautiful. One late-November day found us experiencing both extremes as we carefully made our way along icy country lanes: the sun was shining brightly but at the same time the trees were crusted in such thick rime frost that it looked as though they had been dusted with icing sugar! We were on our way to a tiny village to cater for a funeral tea. Usually funerals are a time of great sadness, but in this case the lady who had passed away was almost 100 years old and she had left detailed instructions about what she would like for her funeral and for the tea that was to be served afterwards. It was to be, in her own words, 'a big party'.

We followed the directions we had been given and were astonished to see where they eventually led us. There, standing beside the marshes was, to all intents and purposes, an old tin hut. We quickly made a phone call to the granddaughter who had booked us to do the catering, thinking that we had made a mistake, but she assured us we were in the right place.

She told us that the little tin hut was, in fact, the village hall and it had occupied a special place in her grandmother's heart as she had attended numerous village fêtes and teas there while she was growing up. She had also enjoyed many cherished memories of playing on the nearby beach as a child during long, hot summer days spent with her much-loved family. Before passing away, she had therefore decided

A grand send-off

that this would be the perfect place for her nearest and dearest to gather and celebrate her long and happy life.

It was bitingly cold, windy and starting to sleet almost horizontally as we quickly unloaded our van, and we could not wait to get inside and warm up. There were several electric heaters dotted about and we switched them all on so that it was soon pleasantly warm and we could get on with making all the sandwiches. When Kev went to fill the hot-water urns, however, he hit a slight problem - he couldn't find a working tap as the tiny little 'kitchen' was in fact a dilapidated collection of ancient units circa 1950! The sorry - looking hot-water heater had loose wires hanging from it and the sink taps had no tops on them, so they were useless too. Thankfully, we had brought an extra urn with us, and we eventually found a tap that miraculously produced running water behind some stacked chairs in the middle of a wall, so we were finally in business!

We were expecting almost 150 guests for a traditional afternoon tea so we had lots to do, but it's the type of catering I always enjoy. Personally I think that afternoon tea has become an almost forgotten pleasure in today's busy world. Nowadays people rarely go to the trouble of making tiny, crustless sandwiches, or baking a variety of dainty cakes and scones anymore, nor do they practice the art of brewing loose - leaf tea. Partly because of its rarity, a traditional afternoon tea makes you feel both a little bit indulged and slightly naughty at the same time, so it has become a treat that never fails to please. So there we were - the sandwiches were cut, the cakes were sliced and the tea was brewed; now all we needed were the people to feed and water! Along with tea and coffee, we had also been asked to provide sloe gin, brandy and port to warm everyone, as they were sure to be feeling chilled after sitting in the church. It was to be served, strangely, in disposable cups. We heard cars arriving, glanced out of the tiny windows and were astonished to see a convoy of prestigious vehicles making its way down the muddy lane. Rolls Royces, Daimlers, Mercedes and BMWs... you name it, all the great and good of Norfolk and from far beyond had turned out to give this well-regarded lady a

A grand send-off

send-off to remember. We ushered everyone in and battened down the hatches as it was by now blowing a hoolie outside. Indeed, we were beginning to think that it would be a minor miracle if the tin roof stayed on! First things first, we soon handed round the tea, coffee and spirits to thaw everyone out before circulating with the food. Needless to say, people were ready for some sustenance; the cold had given them huge appetites, so much so that we even had to make a few extra sandwiches. The dainty little cakes went down a treat too. By this time it did not feel like a wake at all, it was more like a party, which was exactly what the old lady had requested. One of her grandsons had brought along his guitar and he started playing and singing. By the time he began performing one of his grandmother's favourite songs, Van Morrison's 'Brown-eyed girl', the guests were singing and dancing along with the music and even the waitresses were humming and swaying as they kept the sloe gin and brandy topped up.

Everyone was thoroughly enjoying themselves, so much so that at one point someone put a sleepy baby in the grandson's guitar case for a nap. Even this tiny child sensed the heart-warming atmosphere that had been created in this old tin hut in the middle of nowhere and he was soon gurgling away as happy as Larry while his mum joined in with the dancing! By now it was pitch black outside and the first few guests reluctantly started to drift off. Others soon followed, all having to make their way to their cars using torches and the headlights of other cars parked nearby. Some of the cars were chauffeur-driven; the poor drivers must have been frozen through to the marrow, sitting in their cars the whole time, although some of them had popped in for a cup of tea to thaw out when we invited them in.

Ultimately a funeral is, of course, a sad time, but this was a truly memorable occasion. Not only was it a celebration of a long and happy life lived full to the brim, but it also commemorated a remarkable lady in just the way she wanted. Could anyone really ask for more?

A grand send-off

Forces of nature

In the early days of our outside catering business we had been booked to cater for a wedding near Blakeney on the beautiful North Norfolk coast. The day started bright and early, as we had to be at our kitchen to prepare and bake bread for the celebrations later that day. The vans had to be loaded with food, equipment, china, glass and linen, which is always a big job on its own.

Outside catering differs greatly from restaurant catering: if you are cooking in a restaurant or hotel kitchen, everything you need to do your job will obviously be there and waiting. We, on the other hand, have to take absolutely everything we can think of that we may possibly need during the course of the whole day - every pinch of salt, every teaspoon, saucepan, etc. We have to prepare long lists that we check and check again so that hopefully we do not leave anything behind, as that can be a major setback. On this particular day, the refrigerated trailer had been delivered on site the day before and was loaded with wine, which was cooling down nicely, and the cookers and hot cupboards were also at the wedding venue, ready and waiting. Well, so far, so good: the bread was beautiful, the vans were loaded, the staff had started to arrive, and we were all set to head off in convoy to the wedding marquee.

We arrived in good time and everyone got on with his or her respective tasks. The chefs and kitchen staff set up the kitchen and loaded the chiller trailer with food. The waiting staff polished the cutlery and glassware and laid the tables, the drinks staff polished yet more glasses, set up the bar, opened the red wine and did all the other little jobs that no one really notices but which are essential to the success of any event. The marquee was set in a beautiful old pear orchard behind the bride's parents' house and it was the perfect setting for an early autumn wedding. The electrician who had been asked to provide power for the event had also been asked to uplight the gnarled old pear trees with lots of halogen lamps so they would look dramatic later on as night fell and the guests started to make their way home, full of good cheer.

By now it was late afternoon and, as we were not too far from the coast, a sea mist started to roll in. It was about an hour before the guests were due back to begin the wedding breakfast. The disco had arrived and the DJ was doing a sound check, all our equipment was going full steam ahead when, all of a sudden, we were in semi-darkness. As it happened, it had also started to rain. All the lights that had been carefully placed in and under the trees were on a light sensor, so they automatically came on as we lost the daylight - it looked as though we had overloaded the power as a result, but what to do? Panic was on the horizon when Kev decided to have a look to see where the electricity was coming from, as we had not noticed a generator anywhere. Off he went to find the source. Unbelievably, the electricity was coming from the back of a cooker point that was to be found in one of the holiday cottages that were let by the bride's parents. A qualified electrician had carried out this arrangement, believe it or not! We were lucky to be looking at just a power failure and not a full - blown fire! Luckily the electrician was a local chap so he was immediately called out and was able to put things right, minutes before the guests' arrival.

By now the heavens had opened, it was bucketing down and we had stampeding guests who were anxious to keep their finery dry. On with the show! The wedding breakfast went like clockwork; the timings were all spot on, despite the little dramas that we managed to keep from the bridal party for fear of spoiling their day. With the speeches over and dancing in full swing, we were beginning to relax a bit ourselves.

Forces of nature

After all, we only had to lay up a table for cheese and biscuits later on - what could go wrong? We had been asked to provide some local cheeses, fruit and biscuits, along with the bread we had baked that morning and some homemade chutney - all perfect to nibble on later in the evening. The bride's mother had asked beforehand if it would be possible to serve some Brie cheese that had been given to her as a gift from some French wedding guests. She told us she had put it in the outhouse.

When it was time to put the cheese table out, I walked around to collect the Brie and, as I approached the building, I caught a rather strong whiff wafting from the direction of the outhouse. The closer I got, the stronger the smell became, so when I eventually opened the door, I almost keeled over there and then. It was gloriously smelly and quite overpowering. I could see why it had been relegated to the outhouse! The cheese, as it turned out, was unpasteurised and that left me with a dilemma. At the time of this wedding, the whole country was in the middle of a listeria food scare. Pregnant women, children and the elderly were all being advised not to eat any unpasteurised cheese, pâté or raw eggs, and it was obvious we had guests in all those categories.

I knew it would not be possible for me to serve food that I did not know the source of; if anyone became unwell it would put me in a very awkward position. I needed to talk to the mother of the bride, to explain why the Brie would not be on the table. As luck would have it, a few minutes later she came through to the kitchen to thank us for the delicious dinner we had served, and also to let us know how well everyone was being looked after. I explained the problem I had, but she really wanted the cheese served, as the people who gave it to them would think it was odd that it was not part of the celebrations. I could see her point, but I was adamant. We duly laid out the cheese table... minus the Brie. When I returned to the kitchen, the mother of the bride stood there armed with the stinky cheese, ready to put it in pride of place on the table. What happened next was like something out of a Monty Python sketch. She was holding one side, I was holding the other, and neither of us was about to give in any time soon: it was the culinary equivalent of the hokey-cokey - in out, in out, shake it all about!

Eventually I had a brainwave - how about they have the Brie the next day for lunch? I knew they were having guests over for lunch the day following the wedding and I thought there was a possibility the French guests would be among them. If the bride's mother served it then, rather than at the wedding reception itself, everyone would be happy I made my suggestion to the mother of the bride and she thought it was a great idea, so back into the outhouse it went. The rest of the evening went by without any more dramas. The guests made their way home through the beautifully lit pear trees and, an hour or so later, we followed them. A few days after the wedding we received the loveliest letter from the mother of the bride, full of praise and promising us that 'the Brie that had clearly tried to walk out of the catering tent under our very eyes was gorgeous'! All in all, it was another very memorable day.

Forces of nature

A wet and windy day out in North Norfolk

Norfolk is a wonderful place to have a holiday, be it a short break or the luxury of a whole summer spent idling by the seaside. Keen to promote the area, the North Norfolk Tourist Association used to hold a two-day show before the start of each summer season to promote some of the region's attractions. The first day was always a trade show and the second day provided an opportunity for the public to come and see what the area has to offer.

For a few years we were asked to provide the catering for these shows at various different locations... Walsingham Abbey, Wolterton Hall and the North Norfolk Railway, to name but a few. However, the event we remember most vividly is the one that was held at Pensthorpe Nature Reserve. I should mention that Pensthorpe is a beautiful place to visit at any time of the year and for any reason, but its main attraction is the wild birds that come to visit the wetlands. The week before the show at this beautiful venue the weather had been exceptionally wet and windy and the marquee company had the difficult job of erecting two main marquees, as well as a few smaller tents, on the already saturated ground.

We were to be based in one of the main marquees where we would set up a restaurant that would provide hot lunch on the first day for approximately 250 exhibitors and their guests. On the following day we were to run a café to cater for around 500 members of the public. Two days before the show Kev installed all the heavy equipment we

A wet and windy day out in North Norfolk

would need in our marquee, such as cookers, hot cupboards, etc. At that point we were starting to become a little concerned about how soggy the ground was underfoot: it always makes our job that much more difficult when we have to move large quantities of heavy china and cutlery, as well as all the kitchen equipment needed for such a large event, on slippery surfaces. The night before the show, the rain finally stopped but the wind had really picked up. On the day itself, we were all up bright and early to load the vans with food and drink and travel to the venue, although it was still very windy.

Once at Pensthorpe, some of us started work by setting up the kitchen, while others started to lay the tables: later that morning we were due to have a Health & Safety inspection, as well as an Environmental Health inspection, so we wanted to be well prepared. By then, the whole marquee was creaking and gently billowing like a galleon in full sail with the canvasses flapping and the ropes creaking, so it was very unsettling. Just before 11 am the Health & Safety Inspector arrived and started to have a look around to make sure everything was in order. He walked into the marquee along with one of the organisers, looked up... then promptly ordered us all out!

We thought he was joking, but no, he was deadly serious: he deemed it unsafe for us, or anyone else, to be in there. It turned out that because of the continuous strong winds throughout the week, the pegs for the main supporting ropes had worked loose with the constant movement and the whole lot could either collapse or take off at any moment. In fact, soon after, one unfortunate lady was actually in one of the portable loos when it was blown clean over - not something she would forget in a hurry! Thankfully she was unhurt.

After frantic discussions, it was decided it was too much of a risk to carry on with the whole event and it was cancelled there and then. By now people had started to arrive and it was chaos, although the organisers did their best to explain what had happened and why. We were walking around in a state of disbelief when it began to dawn on us exactly what the cancellation meant for us - we had prepared a mountain of food but there was no longer anyone to feed! The organisers told us to do what we wanted with it, or failing that, to throw it all away, although they assured us that we would be fully recompensed for the whole event. Even so, we were bitterly disappointed as we had put in a lot of time and effort and it appeared it was all to be for nothing. Sadly we returned to the kitchen to try and figure out what to do next.

The thought of throwing out perfectly good food did not sit well, so Kev had a brainwave. He made a few quick phone calls and then broke out into a big grin, asking us all, 'What is it they say about every cloud having a silver lining?' It turned out that he had called St Martins Housing Trust, a homeless hostel in Norwich, to ask if they would like a donation of a rather large amount of delicious food! They were delighted to accept and so we took the whole lot to them later that afternoon.

I cannot tell you how much pleasure it gave us as we, along with some of the residents, unloaded the vans and proceeded to stock up all the Trust's freezers and fridges with homemade soups, pies, casseroles and cakes galore - they said it was as though Christmas had come early! As it had all been freshly cooked it was perfectly safe to freeze and be enjoyed over the next few weeks, so they were absolutely thrilled, as indeed were we! Since that eventful day we receive a card from the St Martins Housing Trust every Christmas and, as we open it each year, we are reminded that very occasionally an ill wind does blow some good!

A wet and windy day out in North Norfolk

A day at the races

Quite a few years ago now we were approached to see if we would be interested in running the catering operation for Fakenham Racecourse. We had managed to get our business up and running nicely by then so we thought it would be a challenge to try our hand at something completely new. As it turned out, 'challenge' was the operative word! This was before the racecourse's new Prince of Wales Stand, which now houses the kitchen, restaurant, bar areas and the private boxes, was built.

We were to set up a small preparation kitchen on the ground floor of the building that the jockeys used to stay in, so the facilities were pretty basic. After a good clean and a lick of fresh paint we made the most of what little equipment was already there, before putting in the essentials ourselves. The main kitchen we would be working in on race day was completely separate and was set up a couple of days beforehand in the members' restaurant marquee, where we had installed gas ranges and other equipment to enable us to prepare the hot lunches.

One thing we did inherit was a rather antiquated cooker. The first thing we did was give it a jolly good clean and, once we did that, we thought it was serviceable. Our first race day was upon us before we knew it. We were to provide lunch for the Chairman's private box, as well as running the members' restaurant of about 80 covers in the marquee, and feeding all the jockeys, stable lads, stewards and press. On top of all that we were preparing and serving a corporate event

A day at the races

buffet in an adjoining marquee for about 100 people. Little did we know what we had let ourselves in for! The day before the big day we worked hard preparing the mountain of food that would be consumed on race day. On the menu in the main restaurant was good old-fashioned treacle tart and I had worked out that we would need about a dozen tarts, so we duly made the pastry, put it in the fridge to rest and then got on with the filling. By now it was early evening and we had been working for 12 hours, so we were definitely flagging.

In no time at all we had assembled the tarts and carefully placed as many as we could into the oven. About ten minutes in and there was the most almighty bang, rather like a gunshot. The glass door of the oven had shattered into a thousand pieces, like an old-fashioned car windscreen, all over the tarts We realised immediately that we would have to start again from scratch, but by now it was after 8 pm and we had no cooker! The only thing we could do was take all the ingredients back to our own kitchen and make the tarts again. It was a serious setback. By the time we had returned to the kitchen and eventually finished baking, it was almost midnight and we were all exhausted and apprehensive as to what the next day would bring. The next morning the first job that Kev had to undertake was install another cooker. Luckily we always have spare equipment in storage and so he was able to do the job quite quickly and, after a quick clean, we were back on course.

It was not long before we had a queue of hungry jockeys and stable lads ready for their breakfasts - they needed to load up with enough calories to see them through the day until they could eat again later that afternoon. Boy, could they eat! We were all amazed at how such slim young men could pack it away. While all this was going on we had separate teams of people setting up the buffet lunch for the corporate event, the Chairman's private box and the members' restaurant, so it would be fair to say there was a lot going on! It was almost lunchtime and, having finished with the breakfasts for the jockeys and stable lads, we could concentrate on getting all the food where it had to be at the correct time.

A day at the races

All was going according to plan and we were on schedule. As often the case with these things, when you are feeling quietly confident, a spanner is bound to come hurtling into the works. That particular day the spanner happened to be a power failure. As it was a really busy meeting there were huge amounts of power being used all at once and, as a result, there was a massive drain on the supply. Just as we were about half an hour into the lunch service, the whole course lost its electricity supply. Add to that the fact that it had started to rain heavily and we went from cruising along nicely to the early stages of panic quite quickly! You'll remember that this was our first race meeting so we were a little unfamiliar with what went on, particularly when heavy rain interrupted the proceedings. We certainly hadn't taken into account that the people in the members' restaurant, not wanting to miss a single race, would all rush outside en masse to watch each race as it took place, never minding what stage of their lunch they were at. This resulted in them asking if we could either keep their meals hot, or delay serving them until that particular race was over. It was an operational nightmare for us!

At one point one of the waitresses burst into tears with the stress of everyone trying to get her attention at once, and I knew exactly how she felt. But, as the saying goes, the show must go on. Although we did not have electricity, it did not affect the cooking side of things as we always use gas bottles to run the ranges, but it did mean that we would be unable to serve coffee; unfortunately there was nothing that could be done about that.

The other problem we had was with the corporate lunch. Because it was a casual affair with no set seating, lunch was to be a rolling buffet with guests coming and going. Little did we know that the organisers had continually invited people back and, as a consequence, many, many more people appeared expecting lunch than we had been asked to provide for. They just kept coming! It was like the film 'Zulu', where just as you thought everyone had appeared, another lot came, and another, and another... Luckily, as I said earlier, it was our first meeting so I had been generous when ordering the food requirements, as I

A day at the races

knew the worst thing that could happen was for us to run out of anything. Thank goodness I did, because by some small miracle we managed to perform the old 'five loaves and two fishes' act and no one went away hungry. We estimated that we had fed an extra 50 to 60 people! By now we had managed to serve the Chairman's party of 20, the corporate lunch for 160, about 50 jockeys and stable lads, as well as an eventual total of 100 members as we had picked up a few extras of those on the way.

The light was now beginning to fade but we still had to clear up the aftermath. We did as best we could in the twilight and, just as we had almost finished, power was restored. By this stage we were all absolutely both physically and mentally shattered and longing to pile into the vans to go home, which we all managed to do eventually. We obviously didn't let that first experience put us off as we went on to run the racecourse's catering operation for a further two years and eventually moved into the brand new Prince of Wales Stand, which was officially opened in 2002 by the Prince of Wales himself. I am glad to report that we never did have such a stressful meeting as that first one; it really was a baptism of fire!

A day at the races

Wild life

It was a perfect, late - autumn morning and we were driving along the beautiful North Norfolk coast to prepare the christening lunch for the latest grandchild of a lovely family we know. We duly arrived, unloaded the van and started to prepare in readiness for the guests. Drinks and nibbles were to be served outside to make the most of the garden and the weather, so most of the staff were out there polishing glasses etc.

I was on my own in the kitchen working my way through the list of things I had to do. The front door of the house was open, as well as the back door, and a refreshing sea breeze was blowing through. I was in the most beautiful kitchen and the view out of the windows over the marshes was magnificent so, all in all, it was a pretty perfect day. Then, out of the corner of my eye, I saw a woolly head, followed by an even more woolly body. There in the kitchen doorway stood a sheep. He stared at me as if I was an intruder and I, in turn, stared at him thinking the same thing, not quite believing my eyes.

For a split second I thought I might be hallucinating. After some kind of Mexican stand-off he eventually sauntered through the kitchen and disappeared off through the house. Because he appeared so completely at ease, I assumed he was a pet and probably hand-reared, so I rather foolishly carried on with my list as time was getting on and the guests would soon be making their way back from church. About half an hour later we were in full swing and my confrontation with Larry the Lamb

Wild life

had been forgotten. After copious amounts of champagne had been drunk and nibbles nibbled by the guests, it started to spit with rain and everyone came in en masse for lunch. After the first few guests had helped themselves from the hot buffet we had prepared, they started to drift through the downstairs rooms to find somewhere to sit. Suddenly a cry went up, 'Sheep in the drawing room - how bizarre!'. Then it seemed everyone wanted to crowd in there to see if it was a joke. Well, I can tell you, it was no joke and the poor creature, by this stage, was well and truly spooked.

It was careering around the room in a way that I can only describe as like a motorcycle on the wall of death! The more people crowded in to see the spectacle, the more frightened he became and the higher up the walls he ran. He jumped onto a little table we had laid out with sandwiches and mini chipolatas for the children, split the beautifully embroidered tablecloth in half and proceeded to do a pretty good impersonation of Michael Flatley in 'Riverdance', with sausages flying everywhere! It seemed to me as though the whole spectacle was played in slow motion, although in reality it was only a few seconds.

As you can imagine it was both horrendous for us yet hilarious for the guests. I was truly mortified and I could not believe what had just happened before my very own eyes. Eventually, the gentleman of the house rushed through the assembled guests, calmly grabbed hold of the hapless animal's ear and marched him outside. To the astonishment of all present the errant sheep galloped off over the marshes and back to his friends. It turned out that he was no pet sheep; he had just been grazing on the marsh and decided to gatecrash the party and see what was going on! Then the clear-up began. As discreetly as possible staff began to clear away broken china, glass and other unmentionables left by the terrified beast and sooneverything had been swept up swiftly with a dustpan and brush. To their everlasting credit the staff were so completely unflappable that they just carried on as if it was something they dealt with every day. Later on it transpired that never before had such a thing happened and, at the time of writing, to the best of my knowledge it has not happened since!

Wild life

The lady and gentleman of the house thought it was all great fun and took it as a good omen on the day of the christening. I, on the other hand, felt like lying down in a darkened room with a wet towel on my head!

Wild life

53

All cookers great and small

Over the years that we have been running our catering business we have had to make ourselves at home in many, many kitchens across our part of Norfolk. Sometimes we will provide our own cookers and sometimes we will use the cooker that is in the kitchen where the event is held. When we bring our own cookers we are able to rely on them because we use them all the time. We are familiar with the capacity and temperature, how many of our tins will fit on each shelf, how many saucepans will go on top, etc.

We used to hire various pieces of equipment in when we first started out but they did not always turn out to be reliable, as the following anecdote demonstrates! On this occasion we had hired a gas hot cupboard and we arrived as usual, switched on the gas bottles and got everything up and running. Half an hour or so later Kev went to check to see if everything was working okay and he quickly realised it was not. The pilot light had gone out, so he relit it and switched the main gas jets on. Ten minutes later, he went to recheck that all was well, opened the door... and BOOM!

The gas had built up inside due to a faulty thermal cut-out, and the minute Kev opened the door the air whooshed in and the whole thing exploded. It was the most awful sound; poor Kev was propelled backwards holding his hands over his face. When he took his hands away we could see that he had burnt both his eyebrows and eyelashes off, as well as burning his lips, nose and front of his hair. We quickly

All cookers great and small

put some tea towels in iced water and wrapped them around his face. While all this was going on he kept saying he was just thankful it had not happened to anyone else, but that is typical of the way he is, always putting everyone else before himself.

As a general rule, when I go into a kitchen and I see an Aga, my heart sinks. I know that may be a controversial statement but it is the truth. We have, over the years, had too many Aga sagas to mention. I am completely aware that generally people who have Agas look upon them as part of the family, a bit like a beloved elderly aunt - occasionally cantankerous, not always reliable, but ultimately a warm and comforting presence to have around. I unfortunately feel they are only good for two things - warming your backside on a cold winter's day and drying tea towels! Give me gas and stainless steel any day.

We have had to use ovens that are so seldom used that we have had to de-cobweb and de-spider them before we can cook anything, and even ovens so old that the temperature gauge reads 'cool, warm, moderate, hot, V hot and V V hot'! That last one did make us laugh! One winter's day we went off to cook a lunch for 90 people and we were assured the old cooker would be fired up and ready to go as soon as we arrived. When we got there, the first thing that struck us was how cold the kitchen was. I checked the cooker to make sure it had indeed been turned on. It was a very old Parkray with a small glass door one side and, to my utter astonishment, the glass in the door had been broken and someone had replaced it with a piece of cardboard covered in tinfoil! It had indeed been switched on, but of course we were unable to use it.

It was staggering to think that we were expected to produce braised pheasant, mashed potato and roasted vegetables on such a woefully inadequate, not to mention antiquated, piece of equipment. What to do? The house we were in had another much smaller kitchen up two flights of rickety stairs. Despite the climb, this kitchen had the double bonus of two cookers in it and plenty of room to load all the tins and trays we had to get in. Miraculously we were able to serve lunch on time, but the downside was that it very nearly killed us doing it. By the time we had carried everything upstairs, cooked it, carried it all back downstairs, served it and then taken it all the way back through the house to load in the van, our legs felt like jelly! We can see the funny side of it now, but at the time we were not in the least amused. On another occasion we were asked to provide lunch in a lovely old rectory to celebrate a very rare achievement - the blue sapphire (65th) wedding anniversary of an elderly lady and gentleman who had lived in their house for almost all their married life. When we arrived we were shown to the kitchen and there, on a raised platform, stood in pride of place the culinary equivalent of the Mighty Wurlitzer. It was one of the oldest and largest Agas I had ever seen; it was pillar-box red and looked like a vintage fire engine!

The most incredible thing about it was that when we started to open its doors and look inside, we must have disturbed a family of mice who had made their home in one of the many warming ovens. Before we knew it, there were at least a dozen mice fleeing in all directions, not to mention the waitress I had brought with me... it was absolute pandemonium. The gentleman of the house was in the drawing room reading the Sunday newspapers, oblivious to the ongoing fiasco. I watched one mouse scamper right under his chair and I quietly crept in, armed with a margarine tub to clap down on the little blighter. As if it was the most normal thing in the world, he lifted his legs so I could crawl behind the chair on all fours - it was like a scene from a 'Carry on' film! Luckily I am not in the least bothered by mice and that day I managed to catch and dispatch at least six this way before I even started to get changed into my chef's whites. By now the waitress had gathered her wits and was able to serve the lunch with only the odd fearful glance at the Aga; the poor girl was well and truly traumatised. The whole family, however, was very appreciative of both the catering and rodent removal service we provided!

Another kitchen, another cooker, and another story! This time we were to provide canapés for about 100 guests in a brand new kitchen. When I walked in and saw the cooker it was love at first sight: there in all its gleaming glory this time stood the culinary equivalent of a Rolls Royce! It was a custom-built French Lacanche range, all polished stainless steel and chrome, at a cost of upwards of £25,000. I had never seen anything like it and could not wait to start cooking, but there was a slight drawback...

The gentleman of the house did all the cooking and he was just over two metres (seven feet) tall, so all the worktops and appliances were made and fitted so that he could work comfortably and not have to stoop. This meant that all the surfaces and equipment were so high I had to stand on a bread crate so I could reach everything, including a very powerful wok burner that sounded like a jet engine when I fired it up. It was quite nerve-racking using such a powerful piece of equipment, and at one point I almost did a 'Mrs Doubtfire' and manage to singe the front of my jacket! Later it transpired I was the very first person to cook on that wondrous range, so I felt very privileged. Another time we were asked to cook lunch in a stately home for a small wedding party. We had unloaded and were preparing the first course when Grace, our youngest daughter, came through the kitchen in a hurry carrying a pile of rather expensive plates. I did not notice that a stray mushroom had fallen on the floor when I was frying them earlier. Grace didn't see it either and she 'went for a Burton' as the saying goes. She did the splits whilst miraculously still managing to keep from dropping the plates! Bless her, she narrowly missed knocking herself out cold on the handrail of the cooker, and it was the first time we have had to put a mushroom-related incident in the Accident Book.

On another occasion we had been asked to cook a celebratory Sunday lunch in a small village on the outskirts of Norwich. We had been informed that there was a large old Aga, as well as an electric oven as back-up, if needed. We duly arrived and unloaded. I had an enormous joint of rib of beef, a glorious thing weighing in at just over 11.3 kg. This was to take pride of place on the sideboard in the dining room and I intended to carve and serve it from there, along with the accompanying Yorkshire puddings. The vegetables were to be placed in dishes so that the guests could help themselves. I put the beef in the

All cookers great and small

Aga and then got on with preparing the vegetables. After about an hour, the most delicious smell of roasting beef began to fill the kitchen, but I was starting to worry.

I realised that the Aga was not as hot as the temperature gauge said it should have been. I was going to have to put the electric oven on too, or I would be unable to get everything cooked on time as I had hoped the beef would be out of the oven and resting before I had to put in the Yorkies and roast potatoes. I turned the Aga up as high as it would go, but knew it would take a while before it would be hot enough to get everything cooked. To my horror, when I went to switch on the electric oven, it was not working at all! It was used so seldom that it had not been checked before our arrival to see if it was in good order. Now I really did have a problem! The lady of the house came through and I told her of my predicament. She felt awful that she had assumed the other oven was okay and, after a few minutes' thought, hit on an idea. We could cook the beef in the oven of her next-door-neighbour (a lady who had fortunately been invited to the lunch), leaving her oven free for the other things I had to cook. She quickly popped next door to ask if it would be okay, then returned a few minutes later and said yes, so Kev carefully took the huge joint out of the Aga and staggered next door with it. I was rather relieved, thinking we were out of the woods, but no such luck - the joint was too big to go in the neighbour's oven!

By now I was starting to panic. I really did not know what to do for the best; in two hours' time the guests would be arriving and it was unthinkable to serve roast beef without Yorkies. The lady of the house thought long and hard again, and then she dashed off to make a call. Two minutes later she was back to say she had found another large Aga we could use. The only problem was that it was in her friend's house and she happened to live a few kilometres away in the next village! Unbelievably, we wrapped the joint in tin foil, put it in the back of the van and Kev took it to the next village to finish cooking. It went in the Aga there with no problem, so he stayed with it to make sure it was all right. I stayed where I was and got the rest of the meal prepared and, amazingly, even with all the faffing about, we were still on schedule.

All cookers great and small

The waitresses, bless them, got on without Kev to help with the laying of the tables, as well as all the other little jobs that had to be done to ensure we had no more hiccups. When it was time to bring the beef back, it was like a military operation. Kev appeared with the joint just as I was getting the Yorkshires and roast potatoes out of the now very hot Aga. Even if I do say so myself, it was all perfect, and they were probably the most impressive Yorkies I have ever made!

After all the drama, I went into the dining room and carved the beef to rounds of applause. It looked magnificent but I did have a secret smile as I thought... 'if only they knew'! So you see, we never know what we are going to be faced with when we are out and about cooking in the kitchens of North Norfolk: it's usually Good, it can occasionally be Bad, but hopefully it's not very often that it turns out to be Ugly!

All cookers great and small

Boys will be boys

It was in the early days of our business that we found ourselves agreeing to do a rather unusual event, even by our standards. We had been booked to cater for a themed evening in an old barn for a stag night. The food was to be an approximation of a medieval banquet and all 20 stags were to be suitably attired as monks. We had the greatest fun researching the food, so that we could make it as authentic as possible. It was nice to do something completely different. We decided to prepare a root vegetable soup, followed by a whole roasted suckling pig. To finish there would be raspberry dumplings, all washed down with copious amounts of ale so, all in all, it was destined to be a veritable feast.

The day before the banquet I took delivery from my butcher (should you be at all squeamish, look away now) of the most perfect plump whole piggy. I carefully scored the skin to make the thinnest, most melt-in-the-mouth crackling imaginable, and put him on a large tray in my chiller. I then fashioned a little headpiece out of tin foil so his ears would not become burnt when I put him in the oven the next day. We finished all our preparations in good time. We had also been asked if we could provide all the guests with a hearty cooked breakfast on the morning of the banquet, to set them up for whatever boys do on a stag weekend. They would then be out all day so we would have plenty of time to set up for the evening's dinner. us... it was hilarious.

On the morning of the banquet we took delivery of some recently shot pheasants, partridges and rabbits, all of which were still in feather and fur, along with fruit, nuts and leaves to make a stunning centrepiece for the table. The 'Brothers', as we called them, were to be seated on bales of straw and the whole barn was to be lit by candlelight. I hasten to add that we had fire extinguishers to hand should we be unfortunate enough to need them. When we had finished our preparations we were thrilled with how it all looked and hoped the guests would be suitably impressed too.

I had done my maths and worked out that Mr Pig would need at least three hours in the oven. So, working back from the guests' arrival time of 8 pm, I would need to get him in a ripping hot oven set at 200°C for half an hour at 5 pm to set the crackling all over, before turning down the oven to about 160°C for a further two-and-a-half hours or so. This would allow plenty of time for him to rest while the 'Brothers' were enjoying their first course. So, table laid, pig in the oven, waitresses dressed as serving maids, we were ready... all we needed was the 'Brothers' to make an appearance! Eventually they started to arrive and we were able to get the dinner under way. It was ever so slightly eerie, seeing them all lined up outside the old barn. They filed in, heads bowed, and took their places at the table in silence. The first course went down a treat; they all made suitable noises of appreciation, so once that course was over, it was on to the main event.

The pig - oh what a pig - was all burnished and golden and crispy, complete with a red apple in his mouth, and resting on a bed of bright green rosemary. As I wheeled him in on a wooden cart, he got his very own rapturous round of applause. All fell silent as I began to carve that magnificent beast and, by now, the guests were salivating. It was indeed the most amazing scene, with the beautifully decorated table, laid only with wooden boards and knives (to keep it authentic), and the 'Brothers' in their habits, bathed in the golden glow of candlelight. It is fair to say that they did Mr Pig justice, enjoying second and even third helpings, so that all that was left was a heap of bones and a few sprigs of rosemary. I don't know how they managed it, but they soon after polished off the raspberry dumplings, served by one of our rather well-endowed waitresses, who acquired the nickname 'Sister Luscious Top Shelf'. Then, of course, it was on to the main event at such gatherings, namely the drinking. By now we had finished our part in the evening's events and the waitresses were having a last clear down before we left the guests to it, so to speak. Someone had put some music on and things were getting rather lively, should we say, and we will leave it at that!

Then, just as we were about to leave, one of the 'Brothers' had the bright idea of starting a food fight. Before we knew it, it was more than a fight - it was all-out war and there was food flying everywhere. Luckily none of us got caught in the crossfire and we beat a very hasty retreat. We phoned Kev to come and collect us but, unbeknown to him, the 'Brothers' had heard his van on the shingle and thought we were all leaving without saying goodbye. They all ran out into the kitchen yard and bent over and gave us an (almost) 21-bare-bum salute! Kev said you should have seen the look on their faces when they realised they had all mooned Kev as well as us... it was hilarious. We chuckled about that for days and I must say we were most impressed by the way they cleaned up the barn after their shenanigans... it was spotless!

A couple of weeks later we received a lovely letter from the bridegroom thanking us for the whole evening, but the truth was that it was as much fun for us as it was for him and his friends! I am SO glad we didn't need those fire extinguishers though - that would have taken some explaining to good old Health & Safety!

Boys will be boys

Three wheels on our wagon

Over the past few years, we as a company have gained the reputation of providing both unusual food and the ability to cater in unusual places. Sometimes we even do both at the same time! A few years back we were asked if we would be able to provide a drinks reception to help officially open the recently refurbished theatre that sits almost at the end of Cromer Pier. Several things made that particular event memorable, not least trying to get one much-loved member of our staff actually on the pier in the first place without suffering a panic attack! Poor old Tracy was quaking in her shoes by the time we had got all our equipment unloaded from the van and onto a little cart so that we could wheel it to the very end of the pier without having to carry it all piece by piece.

There were seven of us in our team working that day and it was all very exciting. As we merrily trotted along the pier we were being buffeted from all directions by a bitingly cold wind. Trace was staring straight ahead, quietly turning a delicate shade of green as she tried desperately not to look down and through the gaps in the wooden planks we were walking on. Below us the sea was crashing around the structure's supporting poles and churning up the shoreline into a thick brown foam. After a few minutes we reached the theatre and then the small building perched on the very end of the pier - the lifeboat station. Trace was mightily relieved when we arrived, although still muttering under her breath something about it not being part of her job description! We were to use the lifeboat crew's kitchen to prepare and serve the canapés that would be served at the reception. Luckily we managed to bring all of the equipment we needed in one trip so we could shut the doors to the wind and carry on in relative peace and quiet.

Once in, we quickly got settled into our familiar routine... drinks staff polishing glasses, kitchen staff preparing food, but not, of course, before we switched on the kettle for a hot drink to thaw us out. In due course the guests started to arrive and we were soon in the thick of it. There was a little walkway between the back of the theatre and the lifeboat station and, as it was still very windy, we had to make sure we covered the canapés so they didn't blow off the dishes and into the North Sea, only to be snapped up by the screeching seagulls that were circling above! Amidst all this we were secretly hoping for a little bit of drama regarding the possibility of the lifeboat getting called out in the gusting weather. Not that we were wishing for anyone to be in trouble out there, you understand - a practice run would have been thrilling though! We did keep the crew member who was on duty suitably nourished and topped up with tea just in case! I do think that particular event was especially memorable, not only because the venue was so unusual but also because the weather played a part in bringing home to us just how unusual our job is.

When we had poured the last glass of wine and served the last of the canapés, it was time to pack up all our kit and load up the faithful 'chuck wagon' as it had been christened. We once again wrapped up against the cold wind and trundled off back down the pier, with Trace staring bravely straight ahead, accompanied by a chorus of 'Three wheels on my wagon'.

Three wheels on our wagon

67

Lamb in the van

The Great Hospital in Norwich was founded in 1249 and we have been fortunate enough to cater for many memorable events within its beautiful halls since we started up in business. It's a truly fabulous setting for any event but, it being a medieval building has brought us problems regarding the catering facilities, not least because the kitchen is not much bigger than a broom cupboard! In fact, I have seen much bigger broom cupboards!

Along with its 'bijou' appearance, for some bizarre reason someone had previously decided that the best place to install the smoke detectors was over the cooker! With the very low ceiling in the kitchen, over the years we have had to call out the fire brigade on a few occasions due to the sensitive nature of these detectors as they kept going off all the time. One particular time we were at the Great Hospital to cook a very important dinner for the Bishop of Norwich. It was a gathering of religious leaders from all over the world and originally was to be for no more than 40 guests as the space and facilities were so limited.

We discussed the menu and, as it was springtime, we decided to feature local lamb with a beautiful herb crust, accompanied by homemade redcurrant jelly. Perfect. As the day drew nearer we thought it would be a good idea to check how the numbers were going and ensure that all was in order regarding timings etc, as these things have a habit of changing. All went well until we started discussing numbers. As it was such an important dinner with a very prominent member of the clergy as guest of honour, there had been very few people declining the invitation, so the final number of guests stood at 65.

This posed a pretty major problem for us, as not only was the kitchen not big enough, but the cooker was now far too small to cook the proposed main course of roast lamb. As usual, at these times of great stress, it was Kev who came up with a master plan. Now, just to explain, some of Kev's plans are not so good, but this one pretty much saved the day. The Bishop could hardly uninvite a few guests to make the numbers more manageable, so Kev's idea was that we could pull off the dinner easily if we had another kitchen and more cooking facilities. The plan was that if we took our very large van, we would be able to put a full-size, six-burner commercial gas range in the back of it! Also, as the van was completely racked out, we had loads of room to lay out starters and puddings, so it was a great solution. The day of the dinner approached and we made our way to the venue in the big van as planned.

We arrived in plenty of time and organised which food was to be cooked where... so far so good. The guests duly started to arrive and, after serving them a few canapés, we were ready to serve dinner. Two of the clergy present lived in the next village to us and, as we had catered for several dinners for them, we knew them very well indeed. They were the clerical equivalent of 'Ant and Dec' - great fun and lovely people to boot. The dinner went like a military operation, i.e. very smoothly and without a hitch. As we started to clear things away the two priests we knew came through to the kitchen to say hello and have a peep behind the scenes, as well as to let us know how much they had all enjoyed their dinner, and how well they were being looked after. It was lovely to see them. After a few minutes of chit-chat one of them said that they were both amazed at how we had managed to cook all that food in such a small space with such a tiny oven. To say they were flabbergasted when they were shown our back-up kitchen was a great understatement, but by now they had been suitably lubricated by several glasses of very fine wine and they thought it was hilarious! Cries of 'What? Lamb in the van... well I never!' went up and were repeated over and over again, causing great hilarity among us all. It turned out that they were so astonished at the ingenuity of Kev's plan that they went through and told the other guests.

The next half an hour could have come straight out of a comedy sketch. A steady stream of archbishops, bishops and various grades of clergy, all in their most resplendent attire, came wandering through to the tiny kitchen and 'Lamb in the van - how clever!' was repeated over and over again. All in all, about 25 of them came through to peer into the back of the now-famous van. Eventually, they all went back to the dining room and finished their coffee, before starting to drift off home. We were feeling thrilled at how the evening had gone and, as we put the last few bits and pieces back into the van, the very last thing to be loaded in was the enormous gas bottle that we had taken with us, so they could all enjoy the celebrated 'lamb in the van'!

Lamb in the van

Dogs, dicks and doorknobs

Over the past few years our job has enabled us to cross paths with some very interesting and also quite extraordinary people. Often we are asked to do a single event, then, over the following years, we are asked back time and time again to look after all the family's high days, and occasionally low days, too. One family in particular stand out as being such great, fun - loving people that I had to include them in this chapter. We have catered for their weddings, funerals, anniversaries, milestone birthdays and christenings over many years.

Every time we get a call from them we start looking forward to the event straight away, as we know it will be both a challenge and, ultimately, great fun. Once we had a call from them asking if we were free to provide a very special lunch for a ruby (40th) wedding anniversary. The menu was to be traditional English fare comprising roast rib of local beef, Yorkshire puddings, horseradish sauce and seasonal vegetables, followed by spotted dick and custard.

Forty guests had been invited so we arrived in plenty of time to get the enormous joint of beef in the Aga, as we knew it would take at least three hours to cook. We then got on with all the usual preparations, such as laying the table, polishing the glasses and preparing the canapés, before making the spotted dick, carefully bending each pudding so it would fit snugly in my old oval steamer. Everything was on schedule and the dining room looked spectacular, with vases of the deepest dark blood-red roses everywhere, in keeping with the ruby theme.

Dogs, dicks and doorknobs

The guests had just started to arrive and they too were playing their part in that each and every one of them was wearing a splash of ruby red too.

Well, first things first - by that I mean champagne, and lots of it, accompanied by a few delicious little canapés to get the gastric juices flowing... not too many though as I wanted the guests to be able to do justice to the beef that was to follow. Everyone had arrived by now, along with a varied assortment of dogs, from a sharp little ankle-snapper to a shaggy-haired, enormous wolfhound, and everything in between; we counted 12 dogs in total. They had the run of the place as they dashed about and it was a miracle that the serving staff didn't trip over them.

Kev called everyone in to eat at 1.15 pm promptly, got them all seated and proceeded to serve lunch. As befitting such a beautiful joint of Belgian Blue beef, there was lots of fine red wine to accompany it. In honour of the occasion I had even bought special tins and made the Yorkshire puddings heart-shaped. It was all going down well and there were lots of compliments coming back from the waitresses. Just then the gentleman who was hosting the party came through to say how much he was enjoying it all. As he shut the dining room door behind him we heard a dull thud on the other side of it, but did not think anything of it at the time. He gave me an enormous bear hug, and then asked if he could look inside the steamer as he was eagerly anticipating his pudding. When he lifted the lid he exclaimed 'Well I never - two bent dicks, I have seen one before, but never two joined together!' There is not a lot you can say to that, so I peeped cautiously inside and, sure enough, as they had cooked, the spotted dicks had swollen up and fused together, which was a truly comical sight.

When the gentleman went to return to his guests to tell them about the bent dicks, he grabbed hold of the doorknob, only to have it come off in his hand. The thud we had heard earlier had been the other side of the knob falling onto the polished wood floor. After that, every time Kev or one of the waitresses needed to go in or out they had to knock

Dogs, dicks and doorknobs

first to see if the knob was in place; it was like a comedy sketch and absolutely hilarious! While all this was going on, all the guests' dogs were sniffing and skulking around to see what they could steal. In the end I could stand it no more, so I got one of the bones from the meat and hurled it into the backyard. They went mad to get at it and all ran outside, so I then promptly shut the door behind them.It was then time to serve the spotted dick dessert. By then I had had time to perform some minor cosmetic surgery to make sure it looked presentable and, thankfully, it did not affect the taste - everyone assured me the dessert was delicious! We then started to clear things away and load them in the van ready to go home.

As we drove out of the yard we were followed by the yapping, snapping, yelping pack of assorted hounds, chasing us down the drive. Needless to say, the party continued long after we had left, tired but happy with a job well done. After having such fun, we were already looking forward to the family's next event!

Dogs, dicks and doorknobs

Oh, we do like to be beside the seaside

The sun was shining and we were on our way to the most fantastic setting for a wedding - Burnham Overy Staithe, on our beautiful North Norfolk coast. The marquee had been put up two days before on what is known locally as 'Millionaires Field'. The hire company had delivered all the heavy equipment we required the day before the wedding and we were all set to prepare food for 140 guests.

As we were literally beside the seaside, we had organised a banquet of the finest seafood the area had to offer - wild sea trout, crab, lobster, brown shrimps, cockles and samphire, all served with lemon and watercress mayonnaise, salad and hot, buttered baby new potatoes with herb butter. For dessert we would be serving baskets of local strawberries, which had been picked by my Mum and Dad the afternoon before, accompanied by bundles of sugar-dusted, heart-shaped Norfolk lavender shortbread, tied with lavender silk ribbon, all served with jugs of cold, thick cream. It was quite a feast! It was a swelteringly hot day and we had to make sure our timings were correct, particularly as we had so much seafood on the menu. We knew we could not lay any of the buffet out until the very last minute, or it would be spoiled because of the heat.

We got on with the usual preparations, laying the tables, setting up the drinks and keeping them as cold as possible in the chiller trailer. Suddenly one of the waitresses let out a shout; she had gone to the loo and was greeted by something that could only be described as a water

Oh we do like to be beside the seaside

feature of which Charlie Dimmock would have been proud! We had been blissfully unaware that the water pressure in the area was extremely high, but we knew now as the pipes on the portable loos had been forced apart, causing water to cascade down the steps. We knew that as soon as we heard the church bells ringing, guests would be making their way back to the reception, so it was action stations or, more literally, 'all hands to the pump'! Kev went to his van and grabbed his trusty old tool bag, an item that has helped us out of many a tight spot over the years. Miraculously he was able to rejoin the pipes inside the unit and so managed to stem the tide. As luck would have it, the land on which the loo block stood was slightly sloping down, so the water had a chance to drain away quite quickly.

After he had finished the emergency plumbing job, Kev was filthy so he had to quickly wash and change into a clean shirt that he had inside the van, just as the church bells started to ring. As the first guests made their way from the church along the quay, we were treated to the lovely sight of them in all their finery - top hats and tails for the gentlemen and the most fabulous hats for the ladies in every colour of the rainbow. Everyone was queuing up to get an ice cream from the little van that was parked close by on the staithe and, by the time they reached us, they were suitably cooled down, so we started serving chilled champagne and canapés, which also went down rather well.

By now we knew we had to make a start on laying out the buffet and we worked quickly to get it all out and presented so the guests could enjoy it as soon as possible. Just as we got all the food out, however, there was a last-minute change of plan. The best man's nerves had got the better of him and it was decided to have the speeches before the wedding breakfast and not after, as originally planned, so he could enjoy his food along with everyone else instead of quietly suffering a bad attack of the jitters. As you can imagine we then had to quickly dismantle the whole buffet and return it to the chiller until the speeches were nearing the end, which was altogether very stressful! Luckily it had been decided to have the speeches outside so we could work without being obtrusive and we were able to listen and then decide when it was best to have our second attempt at getting the food laid out. Sadly, a few months before the wedding, the bride had lost her father, so during the whole run-up to her big day, she had felt that there was something or someone missing. She had been very close to him and his presence was greatly missed at her wedding. After listening carefully to the speeches, we knew when the timing was right for us to get all the food out of the chillers for a second time, and it really was quite a splendid sight if I say so myself. The guests did all our hard work justice and within a couple of hours all that was left were loads of shells, stalks from the samphire and discarded ribbon! After the debris was cleared, the party got well under way and the dance floor was filled to capacity with everyone enjoying themselves. A little later the bride came through to the kitchen to thank us all for everything that we had done for her and her new husband.

She was a vision in the most exquisitely hand- embroidered silk couture gown, which was absolutely stunning. I asked her to give us a twirl, so that we could all see her undoubtedly fabulous wedding shoes but, as she obliged, I was stunned to see under this amazing gown the most dirty, worn pair of trainers I have ever laid eyes on! My face must have been a picture! She started to cry, then went on to explain that her Dad had been a writer and that he used to spend a lot of time running when he was thinking about whatever he was writing about at the time. Because she missed him so much, she thought by wearing his favourite shoes, he would in some small part be with her as she walked down the aisle.It was the most touching story and by now she was not the only one in tears. After she had composed herself, she went back to her guests and enjoyed the rest of the evening. We served everyone hot bacon rolls at midnight and finally dropped into bed, exhausted, at about 2.30 am.

Over the course of our working year we cater for many events, some are joyous and some are sad, but this particular wedding will remain in my memory as a bit of both. It was all perfect - except, of course, someone very important was missing.

Oh we do like to be beside the seaside

Mermaid's Brazilian carnival ball

A few summers ago we were asked if we would provide the catering for a big event to raise funds for a renal unit at our local Cottage Hospital in Wells-next-the-Sea. The unit, known as the Mermaid Centre, aimed to provide dialysis facilities for local people and holidaymakers to save them having to go much further afield for life-saving treatment. It was named in memory of Helen Geering, a local lady who was an active fundraiser for charity, and who often used to dress as a mermaid to raise money at events.

The theme of the event was 'Brazilian Carnival Ball' and the aim was to have 500 guests, so it was set to become the biggest event we had catered for to date. We devised a menu that would taste delicious, be in keeping with the chosen theme and also allow us to serve it quickly so that the guests could spend a decent amount of time on the dance floor. Once the menu was agreed we set about organising the logistics of supplying it! Six full-size catering gas ranges were hired in, along with hot cupboards, china, cutlery, linen, glassware and a full-size chiller trailer.

We kept in regular contact with the organiser and each time he telephoned us with the latest update on ticket sales, he was more and more excited: it soon looked like the event would be completely sold out. However, as the ball was scheduled for the end of summer, people had been away on holiday and there was another last-minute rush so, after an emergency meeting, we decided to sell another 200 tickets.

Mermaid's Brazilian carnival ball

As there would now be 700 guests, we had to quickly revise our numbers for hired equipment, staff and food, and it was all quite stressful. Eventually the food preparationbegan! The first thing we did was make 75 pavlova bases to serve with copious amounts of whipped cream and luscious local summer berries, all topped off with pink stargazer lilies and fireworks - yes, fireworks, not pathetic little candles! I figured that if I couldn't go over the top with the decorations for a 'Brazilian Carnival Ball', then when could I?

When the meat delivery arrived we were staggered. It's one thing writing out an order for 160 kg of pork loin, but quite another seeing it in the flesh, so to speak. We anointed the meat with a delicious rub containing oregano, cumin, bay, lime juice and coriander, then put it to sit in the chiller to absorb the flavours before we roasted it very slowly on the day. There was a similar 'oh my goodness' moment when 160 kg of chicken arrived: it was a truly enormous amount of poultry, but we set about marinating it in the traditional Brazilian cane spirit 'Cachaca', garlic, chilli and sour orange juice, with plans to cook it over charcoal just before serving. By now you may have noticed a general theme to my stories and that is, no matter how much you plan ahead and try to eliminate last-minute hitches, the unexpected often happens! Well, this certainly proved to be the case this time. The day dawned bright but very windy and after a fitful night's sleep (I woke up in a cold sweat as I dreamt that I had forgotten to order the potatoes!) our long day began. First we packed and transported the mountain of food and equipment. We had ended up with 50 staff and they knew what they had to do, so we were all set.

First we put the pork in really hot ovens to ensure crispy crackling, and after half an hour the temperature was turned down very low, to gently cook the meat through. A row of barbecues was also lined up ready to cook the chicken, tables were laid, the wine was chilled and the salads finished off. So far so good... all was going according to plan, but we were right on the coast at Burnham Overy Staithe and by late afternoon the wind blowing in from the sea had really picked up. It was relentlessly buffeting our marquee, so we decided to light up the

Mermaid's Brazilian carnival ball

barbecues before the inevitable rain started. Six of our chefs started to cook the chicken just as it started to pour!

The eleven band members arrived and did their sound check: they sounded amazing and were in keeping with the theme as they were almost all Latin American. Boy, could they blast out the music! I hoped no one in the near vicinity was hoping for an early night! By now the kitchen was filled with the most delicious aromas and the chicken was almost finished, so that was a great relief. The poor chefs were well and truly kippered though as the wind had slightly changed direction and had blown the smoke directly over them! They came en masse into the kitchen area where, coincidentally, two very glamorous female singers were changing into their very skimpy costumes. They were a vision in feathers and lace and not much else so, as you can imagine, that cheered the boys up no end! The guests were arriving in their finery and it was all shaping up to be a memorable night. Unusually, people started dancing almost straight away, probably because the music was so infectious.

After an hour we started to serve dinner and, as there were so many hungry people to feed quickly, we had organised four separate buffet stations with corresponding waiting and kitchen staff: it worked like a dream. The guests were called up two tables at a time from each section to collect their chicken, pork or vegetarian option. While they were being served, their salads and accompaniments were being placed on their tables, so as soon as they got back they could start to eat without having to wait. Talk about military precision! After the main course we were ready to serve our 'Completely Over-the-Top Carnival Pavlovas'!

The lights were dimmed as the waiting staff filed in with the spectacular dessert. It was quite a sight, with the blazing fireworks and gorgeous berries that we had dusted with edible glitter: I had figured that there was no such thing as too much sparkle! It all went down really well and after dinner there was a charity auction with fantastic lots going to the highest bidder - a pair of Nelsonian cast iron cannons on timber trucks anyone? How about a Governess cart or a made-to-measure couture dress? Failing that, how about lunch at Westminster with Prime Minister's Question Time thrown in... what am I bid? Due to not inconsiderable friendly rivalry, the lots went for fantastic amounts of money, which all bolstered the final total. By now it was no holds barred on the dance floor and guests and staff alike were thoroughly enjoying themselves. Eventually however the guests departed and we cleared up as much as we could. We had people going in early the next morning to tidy up and the hire company was also due to collect its equipment, so we made sure it was all put together in one place where it could easily be uplifted the next morning.

As we left, we were aware that the wind had picked up even more and the sides of the marquee were flapping and creaking like mad. We arrived home in the early hours and just about collapsed into bed, totally exhausted. During the night there was the most terrific storm, so the next morning we made our way back to Burnham Overy Staithe with deep trepidation. Our worst fears were confirmed: during the night the wind had changed direction and in effect had funnelled straight into the marquee entrance area. The sheer force of the gusts had ripped off the roof as if it was made of tissue paper and apparently it was lying in a field a few hundred metres down the road!

Gingerly we picked our way through the upturned chairs into the kitchen. To our horror one of the main supporting poles had worked loose with the constant movement of the marquee and it had come crashing down directly on to the numerous crates of china we had so carefully stacked together the night before. We were mortified. Thankfully the hire company was very understanding and managed to claim from its insurance company, as did the marquee company who had to obtain a new roof.

From our own perspective we had an extremely lucky escape: if the storm had broken 24 hours earlier the whole event would have been cancelled for health and safety reasons so we would have been left with that huge mountain of food. We would have still been eating roast pork

Mermaid's Brazilian carnival ball

and barbecued chicken well into the New Year! All's well that ends well though, as a fantastic amount of money was raised that evening for the wonderful Mermaid Unit to provide a much-needed local dialysis service.

Mermaid's Brazilian carnival ball

Whoops-a-daisy

Every so often you meet people for the very first time and you know immediately that you are going to get on well. This was certainly the case with a lovely family who had asked us to cater for 160 guests at a summer wedding that was being held at a nearby stately home. After many discussions about the logistical part of such a big occasion, it was time to get down to one of my favourite parts, which is deciding what was to be served for the wedding breakfast. In due course a menu was decided upon and a date put in the diary for a tasting.

At this point I should explain that when we take a booking for a wedding, we like to ask the bride and groom and their parents to visit us a couple of months before the big day to trial the chosen menu. The reason we like to do this is twofold; firstly we get to meet the most important people beforehand, so when the big day arrives with all its accompanying stress levels, we are not total strangers and we all feel comfortable with each other. Secondly, it is very easy to write a fabulous - sounding menu, but sometimes, as we all know, what you end up with on the plate can be very different to what you envisaged. We want clients to feel confident in what we will be serving to their guests, so they can forget about that side of things, safe in the knowledge that they will get exactly what they had in mind.

The day of the tasting arrived. I was in my kitchen early baking bread and carrying out last-minute preparations such as laying the table, etc. In due course the bride, groom and both sets of parents arrived and lunch got under way. As I said, we hit it off straight away: they were a lovely bunch of people and we knew from that first meeting that we were all in for a memorable day. Their guests were to have the very finest of everything we could lay our hands on. They loved the fillet of beef Wellington and all the other dishes I had prepared for them to sample, so after a couple of happy hours, chatting, eating, drinking and planning, everything was agreed and it was time for them to leave.

The big day was fast approaching and all the carefully laid plans were about to become reality. The most beautiful marquee was erected in the grounds of the house, complete with a lining that looked like twinkling starlight, and there was an enormous wooden dance floor. Tables were laid with snow-white linen, gilded china, highly polished glass and the most beautiful fresh flowers. It was a wonderful sight to behold. The plan was to serve canapés and champagne in the magnificent gardens that belonged to the house. We set up a small service area behind the glasshouses, laid a few tables with linen cloths from which to serve drinks, and prepared for the arrival of the guests. The wedding itself was due to be held in a tiny church on the estate. It too was lavishly filled with summer blooms, and soft golden light was streaming through the stained glass windows. In due course we heard the church bells pealing to celebrate the marriage and saw the slow trickle of guests ambling across the perfectly manicured lawns. Meanwhile, we were full steam ahead with the food arrangements. We started to serve the canapés in the stunning surroundings of the walled garden, the champagne was flowing freely and the guests were thoroughly enjoying themselves, as were we.

After a while it seemed that one of the guests in particular was becoming, dare I say it, a little more than merry! It was a really hot day and that, combined with the delicious champagne, had certainly got the better of her. Soon it was time to sit down for the feast that was to follow. Timing is crucial when cooking such a complicated menu - 20 minutes late and hundreds of pounds worth of beef fillet can be easily ruined. The first course was a Norfolk seafood terrine with freshly baked granary rolls, then came the beef Wellington, followed by warm, dark chocolate

Whoops-a-daisy

puddings with homemade caramel ice cream. It all ran like clockwork. By now the dancing had started and the band was in full swing. The lady I mentioned earlier had continued at the same pace at which she had started out, and she was by now rather worse for wear. The guests were thoroughly enjoying themselves due to the fact that the band had started to play Scottish reels and, as they had a caller, almost everyone got into the spirit and joined in... including, the by now very tipsy lady guest.

I should point out that this lady was wearing very high heels as she staggered on to the dance floor. She was very quickly grabbed by a rather enthusiastic Scotsman and flung at great speed up and down. The inevitable happened and she went down spectacularly. What is more, she stayed down. Pretty soon it was obvious that she was badly injured, as after about ten minutes she was still unable to get up. The dancing was stopped and Kev took the decision to call for an ambulance as her foot was lying at a most unnatural angle and she said she couldn't feel it at all.

While waiting for the ambulance to arrive, she continued to numb the pain by drinking champagne straight out of the bottle, before she was placed on a stretcher and taken to hospital, accompanied by her husband. Once this particular drama was over, we carried on. We were due to serve bacon rolls at mid- night so we concentrated on doing just that. As we were filling the rolls, one of the guests happened to walk into the kitchen to see exactly where the delicious smell was coming from. This guest happened to be a very handsome young Scotsman, complete with kilt, who also seemed to be enjoying his hosts' hospitality to the full. He was a real charmer and he told us how much everyone had enjoyed the dinner we had served them. Laughingly, one of the waitresses asked if it was true what they say about a Scotsman wearing nothing under his kilt. Without batting an eyelid, he promptly grasped the hem of his kilt in both hands and lifted it up almost to his head! To say we were flabbergasted was putting it mildly; we could not believe what he had just done! It's a good job we are not easily shocked, and we all fell about laughing. Unfortunately for him his wife

Whoops-a-daisy

chose that exact moment to follow him to see where he had gone, as apparently this was his party trick whenever he had had a few too many. The poor woman was horrified and gave him a verbal lashing before demanding he cover himself up to avoid embarrassing himself further. She was so angry with him she insisted that they were leaving, so he never did get his bacon roll after all!

After recovering from the shock, we carried on with the bacon rolls until the early hours, and the guests started to leave. We even had a little dance ourselves, as the bride's mum came through and asked us to join them. It had been a long day but it was one of the most memorable weddings we have ever experienced, for all sorts of reasons! Looking back, I think it was the beautiful venue, brilliant guests, the very finest food and drink, and great music that combined to make it all so special. They were a lovely family and it was a pleasure to be asked to be part of the celebrations.

Whoops-a-daisy

Wild, wild west Norfolk

One of the best things about our work is that although we are there to do a job and provide a service, very often we are lucky enough to feel included in the fun too! One such event was the 21st birthday party of the son of one of our regular customers. The theme of the party was 'Wild West Saloon Ball' and we were asked to provide dinner for over 300 guests in an enormous marquee on the family's estate.

All the guests were to be in fancy dress and there would be a DJ, cocktail bar, shooting gallery, casino, bucking-bull machine and, last but by no means least, can-can dancers! It was just the kind of thing we love doing and we could not wait for the day of the party to arrive. We had the usual pre-party meetings to discuss the menu, drinks, timings etc, and we were asked if all our staff would like to participate by dressing up too. It was decided very quickly that they would wear checked shirts and jeans, and that Kev would be 'The Law Man' (naturally), complete with sheriff's badge. I, for some reason, would cook dinner dressed as Minnie Ha Ha! We had a whale of a time picking out our attire and all the fancy dress hire companies in the area undoubtedly did a roaring trade: pretty soon they had nothing left relating to the 'Wild West'.

Time flew by as we were really busy with events right up until the week before the party and, before we knew it, it was time to start the preparations. We had hundreds of tiny tartlet cases for canapés, as well as numerous other time - consuming nibbles to prepare, quite

Wild, wild west Norfolk

apart from the main course, vegetables and puddings! All in all, it was a veritable mountain of food to tackle and transport to the venue ready for the final stages of cooking and serving. Pretty soon the big day was upon us. We started bright and early by being in the kitchen at 7.30 am to bake an assortment of bread. By 10 am the bread was cooling nicely and the kitchen smelt delicious, so there was time to grab a quick bacon sandwich and mug of coffee. Then there were last-minute checks to make sure we had everything we needed on the equipment lists: we double-checked everything before loading it carefully into the vans. This part of the proceedings is very important as it can be a real problem if we forget anything at all, since we are very often miles from the nearest shop. On one occasion we had to send someone back to pick up teaspoons and saucers, which resulted in an incredibly stressful 60-mile round trip, so we are understandably always extra-cautious at this point in the planning.

Once we had everything on board, the staff started to arrive and we set off in a convoy of vans, trailers and cars in plenty of time to allow for traffic hold-ups, which can be frequent during the holiday season in our part of the world. In due course we arrived at the venue and proceeded to unload the cookers, hot cupboards, china and hundreds and hundreds of glasses, not to mention all the table linen and cooking equipment that was required to provide dinner for over 300 hungry guests.

Once we had set up the kitchen, the front of house staff went out to put the cloths on, then lay up the tables, etc. The bar staff put all the drinks that had to be cooled into our chiller trailer, although it was already almost half full of food, and they polished the glasses and uncorked the red wine. By now the DJ had arrived and was doing a sound check so it seemed the perfect time to grab a quick break and have a bite to eat as we would not get another chance until much later that evening. As we were arriving earlier, we had noticed that an old-fashioned 'Wild West' wagon had been positioned at the entrance to the marquee, so we decided it was time for a photo opportunity. We all got changed into our various outfits, then piled into and around the

Wild, wild west Norfolk

wagon to create a really great picture. There were about 20 of us and we certainly looked a motley crew! Soon after that the guests started to arrive: they were a varied and glamorous assortment of cowboys, Indians, good-time gals, Mexicans, sheriffs, squaws and ladies in huge crinolines. They all looked brilliant! The drinks started to flow, accompanied by plenty of canapés to mop them up. We had a job on our hands to get the guests through to the marquee to sit down, so in desperation two gentlemen got a large piece of rope and corralled them through in true 'Wild West' style!

As we proceeded towards dinner, however, there was an unexpected turn of events. The enormous marquee was powered by electricity coming from two generators, but unfortunately, just as we got everyone seated, they ran out of diesel. All the lights went out, but the funniest thing was that the enormous inflatable cacti that were placed throughout the marquee started to collapse and fall on the seated guests. It was like an episode of 'It's a knockout! The waitresses and bar staff were dodging here and there trying their best to push falling cacti away from the bemused guests - it was absolutely hilarious. Eventually, after a frantic few minutes of battling with the man-eating plants, calm was restored... along with the electricity!

We managed to get the main course and pudding served without any further mishaps. By then the guests were ready to take to the dance floor and to enjoy the various sideshows that had been laid on. It was just a wonderful atmosphere and seeing the guests thoroughly enjoying themselves is certainly one of the best parts of our job. We did have a rather unusual request from one of the young men though: he had been dancing so heartily that the sole of his shoe had fallen off, so he asked if we had any glue to stick it back on. We didn't, but Kev had the next best thing - a spare pair of shoes that happened to be the correct size 11, so he lent them to him! He wasn't expecting to see them again, but they were an old pair anyway so it wouldn't be the end of the world if they were not returned. We started to clear away some of the equipment and have a regroup, as our part was not yet over. About half the staff finished at around 1 am but the rest of us stayed on to serve breakfast at about 6 am to the remaining guests. You can imagine that by then we were just about all in as we had had an incredibly long and tiring day, even though we had enjoyed every last minute. We even managed to have a dance ourselves at about 4am behind the coffee table... I think hysterical tiredness was setting in by then! As we drove home we noticed that people had started to set up their stalls at the local car boot sale as the time was by now 7.30 am, a full 24 hours after we had started our shift. We were too tired to look for any bargains that morning, as you can imagine!

When we returned to the venue later the next morning we were astonished to find Kev's old shoes carefully placed at the entrance to the kitchen area, along with a thank-you note for the loan of the shoes that had enabled the recipient to dance the night away! All in all it would be fair to say that 'Wild West Norfolk' had hosted one of its finest parties that night, enjoyed by all who attended, including the staff!

Wild, wild west Norfolk

Our American road trip

After a long, hot, busy summer, Kev and I decided it was time for a break. Earlier that year my Auntie Anna and her son Jim had come from America to visit all our family here, and after their whirlwind trip, we promised one day we would visit them. Four of my aunts married American servicemen and we have a large extended family scattered far and wide across several states: Pennsylvania, Montana, Florida, California and Alabama. We decided to visit Auntie Anna in Pennsylvania and also my cousins Dave and Marilyn in Montana. After firming up our travel plans, we had a few excited weeks before embarking on our Great American Adventure.

Upon our arrival in New York, we picked up our hire car at JFK airport. As you can imagine, the mid-morning traffic was unlike anything we had ever seen. Add to that major roadworks, temporary signage, and a sat-nav having a meltdown, it was inevitable we should find ourselves well and truly lost. At one point we were driving down Madison Avenue, which was absolutely not where we wanted to be! Finally, Kev managed to negotiate his way back onto the right track and after a few hours of uneventful driving (thank goodness) we arrived in Pennsylvania. It was so nice to see Auntie Anna again. She is my mother's younger sister and so like her in every way.

The next day we woke up very early. Auntie Anna wanted us to rest and recover from our journey but we couldn't wait to get out and about. She told us that in Lancaster County, a few miles away, there was a farmer's market and boot sale that day. We decided we had to go, we skipped breakfast, piled into the car and headed off. Pennsylvania is the most beautiful state: farming country, with rolling green fields, and row upon row of carefully tended crops. It has a large Amish community and the local Root's Market is full of the most glorious produce. All grown and cooked by them, and other local producers. It was a lovely sight to see horse-drawn buggies lined up with the horses having a cool drink in the shade.

After entering the main food hall, we were agog. What a treat it was, everywhere you looked, food, food, food! The most fantastic array of sticky pastries, fruit pies, perfect peaches, piles of white sweetcorn with bright green husks, glistening jars of golden honey and watermelons bigger than bowling balls. Seeing all this made us hungry, so we looked around for somewhere to sit and have a late breakfast. We saw a sign that read "Dan's Paper Plate" so we went in.

Soon we were seated and shown the day's menu. As the market was only there one day a week, the food was cooked from scratch that morning and when it sold out, that was it. The waitress had mentioned to Dan we were from England, so Dan came out to say hello and we chatted for a few minutes before tucking into a late breakfast. After we had finished eating Dan came back out to check that we had enjoyed our breakfast, and Auntie Anna told him about our work on the Royal Sandringham estate. Being a fan of the Royal family he was interested in hearing all about our work there, but he soon disappeared back into the kitchen saying, "Sit tight, I'd like you to try something."

A few minutes later, the waitress brought out little samples of all the things that were on that day's menu. They were all delicious but one in particular stood out - his ham and bean soup. I told him how delicious his soup was, and jokingly said it would go down a treat with our customers at Sandringham after a long winter walk in the woods. I then cheekily asked him if he would possibly share the recipe with me so we could put it on our menu. He was happy to do so and we promised to get in contact with him when we got back home.

After lunch we went outside to look at the car boot sale, and I wandered off on my own. After almost an hour, Kev phoned to ask where I was. I met up with him shortly after and explained to him, to his amazement, that I had spent the entire hour at a stall selling - of all things - secondhand cast iron skillets! Grizwold skillets are THE skillets to own (apparently). They have an enormous following of people who collect rare examples and they can change hands for thousands of dollars. The stall holder told me he had such a large collection, that he'd had to reinforce the floor in his basement where he keeps them! I had a full hour's crash course on everything skillet-related: how to tell the run-of-the mill ones from the valuable ones, the stamps on the bottom, the different shapes and sizes of handle. I loved every minute!

On our way to visit Auntie Anna's son Jim and his wife Katy, we decided we had to take a slight detour to see the capital city, so Kev drove Auntie Anna and myself to Washington DC. After an open-top bus tour, we had worked up an appetite and practically demolished our chicken dinners and followed them up with a neon coloured snow cone! We continued our journey to Delaware where Jim and his wife Katy live. We had a lovely couple of days with them, including a day's fishing in the bay at Lewes. That evening we went to a restaurant called Jerry's Seafood, where Jim insisted we try the Crab Bombs. Hands down, they were the best crab cakes I have ever eaten, anywhere. Packed full of blue crabmeat, they were both crispy and creamy at the same time and so large we all shared them; they were truly delicious.

We were nearing the end of this leg of our trip, and Auntie Anna gave us a special send-off because for our last afternoon with her, she had arranged a surprise tea party and invited some of her family and closest friends to join us. Auntie Anna is so like my Mum - including the way she makes her sausage rolls! I spent Sunday morning sitting in her kitchen watching her make them. It was uncanny how she rolled

Our American road trip

the pastry and forked the edges, just like Mum. Her table was groaning with - of course - her amazing sausage rolls and apple pie, as well as the most enormous shoo-fly pie, and sticky buns bought at the market the day before. We had a memorable afternoon-and drank enough tea to float a battleship!

Back home a few weeks later I e-mailed Dan. He, in turn sent me back the recipe, complete with photos. I then spent a couple of days gathering the ingredients, made a batch and needless to say we sold out within a few hours. Our regulars loved it! I told Dan we called his soup 'Dan's Hearty Pennsylvanian Ham and Bean Soup' Soon his regulars back at the market were coming in to ask for what they called "The Queen's Soup," and Dan had to make gallons every week - it even made the local news! Over the winter months the soup became a firm favourite with our regular customers too, and at the end of the winter we sent him our hand written menu board as a keepsake.

We continued to keep in touch, swapping recipes and menu ideas, and it was great fun. Dan and Steven, his partner, had said they had always wanted to come to England. Kev and I decided to ask if they would like to come over for a couple of weeks and see where we live and work.

Almost a year after our first meeting, they came to visit. We had an unforgettable time, showing them where we live and what we like to do. We took them to Cromer to see the End of the Pier Show, and to eat fish and chips and ice cream. We wandered around Norwich Cathedral and Sandringham House, and we met up with family and friends who live along our beautiful Norfolk coastline. And of course we had to have a day-trip to London. After a bright and early start we arranged to meet our daughters, Amii-Rose and Grace, at Kings Lynn train station where they would join us for the family tradition of a bacon roll and coffee before we jumped aboard. The first thing we did on our arrival was head off to Buckingham Palace, and a walk down the Mall for that must-have photo opportunity. By then we had all worked up a pretty good appetite, so we piled into a taxi and set off to the Cafe Royal,

Our American road trip

where we had booked a surprise afternoon tea. After being seated in the jewel box that is the Oscar Wilde Lounge, our table was laden with delicate bone china, cups, saucers as well the most delicious array of savoury morsels. Delicate little finger sandwiches and sausage pinwheels, alongside miniature savoury muffins - complete with pipettes of tomato juice to squeeze in them. Next up, scones as light as air, with thick clotted cream and strawberry jam. Best of all though - for me anyway - were the delicate little cakes, piled onto gilded cake stands; they were miniature works of art. Needless to say there was not a lot left of anything by the time we left our table! We finished the day with an evening trip on the London Eye. It was spectacular to see the lights of our capital city in the twilight, twinkling and stretching as far as the eye could see. We had to dash to get the last train back to Kings Lynn. We had had such a hectic day, trying to fit everything in that we had planned to do, that by the time we had settled into our seats, homeward bound, with the gentle rocking of the train, it wasn't too long before most of us were fast asleep. In truth, we enjoyed a mini holiday too. It's true what they say about not always appreciating what you have on your own doorstep.

Dan and Steven planned their trip to coincide with a wedding we had been asked to cater for. The Bride was Zoe, a family friend, marrying Rowan in a beautiful old barn a few miles from where we live, we thought it would be great fun for them to see behind the scenes at an English country wedding. Zoe had worked with us for quite a few years and so had chosen her "Greatest Hits" from all the past weddings and events she had helped at, including legs of local lamb marinated and cooked over charcoal; her very favourite dish.

The wedding was perfect in every way: beautiful bride, amazing weather, lovely location and great guests. Steven helped behind the bar and Dan in the kitchen. Steven didn't realise at first that Pimms isn't usually served neat so the event got off to a flying start! It was all go, go, go, from the moment we arrived, and such a memorable, happy day for everyone. It was nice for us to show them both our real working life.

Their visit was over all too soon. To finish off their trip we went to our Cafe at Sandringham to have roast beef and Yorkshire puddings, which they absolutely loved. We bade them farewell and vowed to keep in touch, which we have, continuing to swap recipes, photos, and food ideas.

Back in America, after Auntie Anna's stupendous tea party the time had come for us to leave Pennsylvania and begin the next stage of our American Adventure: part 2 would be Montana - the Big Sky Country!

Our American road trip

Our American road trip. Part 2

After a long flight from JFK via Minneapolis, we arrived in Missoula, Montana. Waiting for us at the airport were my cousin Dave and his wife Marilyn, who we hadn't seen for a very long time. Dave's mum Barbara and my mum were sisters, and sadly they are no longer with us. Just like Auntie Anna, Auntie Barbara was like my mum in so many ways. They loved being homemakers - in fact liked nothing better than looking after their families.

It was late at night and we were so tired we could hardly keep our eyes open. After half an hour we arrived at Dave and Marilyn's beautiful home built on the side of a mountain; collapsed in bed and slept like logs. In truth we had no comprehension of just how far we had travelled, but flying from New York to Montana took longer than the flight from Heathrow to New York.

As we had arrived late at night after a long days travelling, we had no real idea of what to expect when we woke the next morning. When we pulled back the curtains we were met with the most jaw-dropping view imaginable. The surrounding mountains, tinged with purple, pink, blue and green rose spectacularly all around as far as the eye could see - Montana really does live up to its name "Big Sky Country", and we really did have a room with a view! After a long breakfast whilst watching the wild turkeys drinking out of the birdbath, we headed off into the woods. Marilyn explained that we were in bear and mountain lion

Our American road trip. Part 2

country so we had to be aware of our surroundings at all times. With both of us feeling more than a little jittery and their dog Willow leading the way, Marilyn, Kev and I, headed off for the most spectacular walk imaginable. Just perfect after all the hustle and bustle of airports, people and travelling in general.

Once we had settled in and had a good catch-up, we set about planning what we were going to do over the next few days. To our surprise, Dave and Marilyn had planned an overnight trip to Glacier National Park, which is situated in Northwestern Montana on the US/Canada border, so we packed a few things and were soon on our way. The journey to the park was so beautiful that words can hardly describe it - Mother Nature at her very best. Just when you thought it couldn't get any better, you went round the next hairpin bend and there was yet another amazing view. We drove on what is called "The Going To The Sun Road". It took us to the highest point on the glacier that you can walk to. When we started at the bottom it was sweltering hot but when we reached the top, much to our amazement it was snowing. You could tell Dave was a local; he was the only one walking around in shorts, oblivious to the cold.

As soon as we arrived we were shown to our rooms in Mountain Lake Lodge, Bigfork, overlooking Flathead Lake, where we were staying the night. After a simple supper and a good night's sleep we headed to one of Dave's favourite places for breakfast. Opposite the lodge there was a gas station with a diner attached called "Woods Bay Grill". We feasted on corned beef hash and blueberry pancakes the size of small pillows: all washed down with mugs very of strong coffee.

We soon got back on the road and drove along Flathead Lake, which is enormous with an incredible 185 miles of shoreline. Cherries are grown on the East side of the lake and vines on the West. As cherries are my very favourite fruit we vowed to return in cherry season. On the way back we took a detour so that Dave could introduce us to John and his partner Syndi. John is a real-life cowboy, he showed us his

Our American road trip. Part 2

mum's, dad's and grandparents' saddles, lovingly polished and proudly displayed. Rodeo is big in Montana and equally popular is the sport known as mutton busting. Believe it or not, kids as young as five happily mount the lively sheep before being let go into the ring, so it's a bit like rodeo for kids!!!

John and Syndi are volunteers for the Montana Water Fowl Foundation, a non-profit organisation dedicated to the conservation and propagation of native waterfowl and their habitat. They work closely with the Salish Kootenai tribe to reintroduce birds that were hunted to extinction, with particular focus on the Trumpeter Swan. In the time we were there we were privileged to see several of these beautiful birds and it was lovely to see the effort being put into protecting them for future generations. On our way back to Dave and Marilyn's house we visited the Mission Mountain Wilderness, not far from John and Syndi's home, where we drove through vast plains dotted here and there with families of buffalo. We stopped to get a better look, but until one of the big bulls came wandering up right beside our vehicle, I didn't really have a clue just how enormous these magnificent creatures are. He could have just flipped us over as if we were in a Dinky toy. After a long hard stare - from him, not us - he sauntered off to join his family.

On our arrival back home we noticed the rubbish bins were knocked over and their contents were scattered all over the yard. Turns out the local black bears are partial to the smell of beer and it's not uncommon for them to wander down from the mountain of an evening to see if there is an odd can they could help themselves to!

The following day we were to go fishing for bull trout on the Blackfoot River. After a hearty breakfast of biscuits and gravy at the Stray Bullet, we loaded up the fishing gear, bought our fishing licences as well as a selection of flies and headed down to the river for a relaxing afternoon's fly fishing. Needless to say we didn't catch a single thing but had the most enjoyable time, standing in the crystal clear water hopefully giving the impression that we had some idea of what we were doing!

Our American road trip. Part 2

After a stroll around the University of Montana campus the next morning, we stopped off for lunch at another of Dave's favourite haunts in Missoula, where we had the most amazing burgers. After lunch we called in at the local supermarket where the quality and variety of food was something to behold. Everything that could possibly be organic and free range was. It was an absolute delight to see the perfect displays of top quality produce. We couldn't resist a beautiful piece of local rib of beef which we planned to have for our lunch the next day. Then on to a shop called "Rockin Rudy's which had everything cherry-related: chutney, pickle, barbecue sauce, ice cream syrup, all made from the local Flathead Lake cherries. I just had to buy some to bring home with me.

After almost three weeks without cooking I was feeling withdrawal symptoms, so I cooked us all a traditional Sunday lunch with that lovely rib of beef and all the trimmings. When we were packing to go on our trip, we particularly wanted to take Dave something unusual as a gift, so we brought him a Yorkshire pudding tin and the plain flour just to be safe! I know Dave and Marilyn love Yorkshire puddings and probably hadn't had them in a while so we spent Sunday morning making them together for our lunch. I have to say they were spectacular! Dave said it reminded him of when his mum used to make them many years ago. Together we also made sausage rolls which we ate WITH our roast beef lunch, and we found out after we had been home a few weeks that Dave had become a dab hand with both the Yorkies and the sausage rolls!

I suspect we could not have chosen two more contrasting places to spend our time. Just seeing the places where our family live, meeting their friends and doing with them the things they themselves love to do was a joy. It was also fascinating for me to see new ways of preparing and cooking food; seeing how to get the perfect crisp coating on buttermilk fried chicken from a lady at the Amish market, how to make a mean sausage gravy to go with fluffy biscuits and trying to find out what exactly WAS in that fiery Mexican sauce that my cousin Dave

Our American road trip. Part 2

so loved. I also couldn't wait to try a recipe I pinched from one of Marilyn's cookery books. Called "Chicken Wiggle" the name made me laugh out loud. How could I not make it?

Sadly our time in America had come to an end. We were bowled over by the warm welcome, friendliness and hospitality we received without exception, everywhere we went. So much to see, eat, do, and discover in such a short time, we will just have to return in cherry season!

Our American road trip. Part 2

Recipes

Quince jelly

Makes 10 x 190g jars

Quince jelly ingredients

2 kg quinces

Juice of 2 lemons, or

2 tsp citric acid 3 litres water

Granulated sugar

Quince jelly method

1. Scrub the quinces, cut into small pieces and put in a pan with the lemon juice or citric acid, and 2 litres of the water. Simmer until tender, then strain for 15 minutes. Return the pulp to the pan with the remaining water, and simmer for another 30 minutes. Strain and mix the two batches of juice.

2. Measure the juice, bring to the boil and add 450 g of sugar to every 750 ml of strained juice.

3. Setting point is (105 ° C/220 ° F). If you do not have a thermometer, place three or four small plates in the fridge when you start to cook the jam. After the mix has been boiling for several minutes, place a teaspoonful on a cold plate and return to the fridge to allow to cool. Remove the rest of the jelly from the heat source while you are testing the setting point.

4. Push the cooled jelly gently on the plate with your finger. If it wrinkles on the surface and the jelly doesn't flow over where you have drawn your finger, its setting point has been reached and the jam has been boiled for long enough. If it hasn't reached this state, re-boil the jelly for a few minutes and try again until you have the desired result.

5. Pour into sterilized, dry jars and screw on clean, dry lids straight away.

Retain the pulp from the quince jelly for the quince membrillo recipe on page 98.

Quince Membrillo

Quince Membrillo method

1. Sieve and weigh the pulp left over from the quince jelly recipe and mix it with an equal quantity of granulated sugar.

2. Place in a heavy bottomed saucepan, bring to the boil and stir until the paste leaves the side of the pan. Turn it to the lowest setting. It will spit and splutter, so cover your hand with a cloth and stir the paste continuously.

3. Add the mixture to a shallow tray lined with non-stick baking parchment and leave in a warm place for 3–4 days. It will keep for up to a year, well wrapped in waxed paper, baking paper or foil.

4. Membrillo is especially good with Manchego cheese, a strong cheddar or blue cheese.

Membrillo ingredients

Pulp from the quince jelly recipe

Granulated sugar

Pavlova

Serves 10 generously

Meringue ingredients

4 medium egg whites at room temperature

225 g caster sugar

1 tsp cornflour

1 tsp vanilla essence or paste

1 tsp of lemon juice

Filling ingredients

290 ml double cream, lightly whipped

450 g fresh, mixed soft fruit

Method

1. Heat the oven to 140 ° C/275 ° F/Gas Mark 1.

2. Line a baking sheet with baking parchment.

3. Whisk the egg whites until stiff and gradually add half the sugar. Then fold in the remaining sugar with a large metal spoon, so as to retain as much of the air that you have incorporated as possible.

4. Fold in the cornflour, vanilla and lemon juice.

5. Place half the mixture on to the prepared baking sheet and shape into a 20 cm circle.

6. Place the other half of the mixture around the edges to form a wall and bake for 1½ hours.

7. The meringue will be ready when the top is a pale golden colour and hard to the touch. Remove from the oven and leave to cool on a cooling wire.

8. When completely cold, place on a serving dish and top first with whipped cream and then the fruit.

9. There is no need to add sugar, as the meringue and fruit should be sweet enough.

Duck with damsons and oranges

Serves 4

Ingredients

4 duck legs

Salt and pepper

200 g damsons - use plums if you can't get hold of damsons

4 tbsp water

2 oranges, segmented and zested

2 tbsp of Seville orange marmalade

2 tbsp port or orange liqueur

Parsley sprigs to serve

Method

1. Preheat the oven to 180 ° C/350 ° F/ Gas Mark 4.

2. Carefully dry the duck legs with kitchen roll and season with salt and pepper, before allowing to come to room temperature.

3. Place the stoned damsons or plums together with the water and orange zest in a small pan.

4. Simmer gently with the lid on for 10 minutes or until the fruit starts to soften.

5. Take off the heat and add the marmalade, port or orange liqueur and orange segments. Set aside.

6. Place the duck legs in a shallow roasting tin and roast for approximately 25 minutes until golden brown and crispy.

7. Remove from the oven, cover loosely with foil and allow to rest for 10 minutes.

8. Gently reheat the sauce and serve with the duck alongside some crispy roast potatoes and a parsley garnish.

Luscious lemon cake

Serves 12

Ingredients

225 g sunflower Margarine

350 g caster sugar

225 g self-raising flour

4 large eggs

4 tbsp milk

Zest of 3 lemons

125 g caster sugar for the syrup

Juice of 3 lemons for the syrup

Method

1. Preheat oven to 170 ° C/350 ° F/Gas Mark 4.

2. Line a 20 cm springform cake tin with baking parchment. Alternatively, use a greased ring tin.

3. In a mixing bowl place the margarine, 350 g caster sugar, flour, eggs, milk and lemon zest.

4. Mix for 2 minutes, or until you have a smooth batter.

5. Pour the batter into the tin and place the tin in the oven.

6. Bake for 40-50 minutes (30-40 minutes if using a ring tin) or until a skewer inserted into the cake comes out clean.

7. Leave to cool in the tin for 20 minutes.

8. Make the syrup by placing 125 g of caster sugar and the juice of three lemons in a small saucepan, heating gently until the sugar has dissolved.

9. Prick the cake all over with a skewer and carefully drizzle the syrup all over it.

10. Leave to cool in the tin. This luscious cake can also be drizzled with icing if required.

11. This is delicious served hot as a pudding with custard or cold as part of a traditional afternoon tea.

A gluten-free version of this delicious cake can be made by replacing the self-raising flour with gluten-free bread flour and 1 tsp gluten-free baking powder.

Country terrine

Serves 10

Ingredients

225 g fresh chicken livers

2 tbsp brandy

½ tsp ground white pepper

225 g streaky bacon, very thinly sliced

1 medium onion, finely chopped

10 g butter

450 g pork belly, minced

225 g chicken thighs, minced

2 cloves garlic, finely chopped

2 small eggs, beaten

Fresh thyme leaves, chopped

¼ - ½ tsp ground allspice

¼ - ½ tsp ground cloves

Salt and freshly ground pepper

Freshly ground nutmeg

50 g hazelnuts and walnuts, chopped

175 g - 225 g cooked ham, cut into thick strips

1 bay leaf

Continued on page 117.

Country terrine

Method

1. Preheat the oven to 180 ° C/350 ° F/Gas Mark 4. Wash the chicken livers, separate the lobes and remove any trace ofgreen. Marinate in the brandy and ground white pepper for 2 hours, and set aside.

2. Line a 1.7 litre capacity lidded terrine (or casserole) with thinly sliced bacon, keeping back a few slices for the top.

3. Sweat the onion gently in the butter until soft, but not coloured. Allow to cool then mix it in a bowl with the minced pork and chicken thighs, garlic and eggs. Add the thyme leaves, allspice and cloves, and the brandy from the marinated chicken livers.

4. Season with salt, pepper and nutmeg. Mix thoroughly. Fry a little piece of the mix and check the seasoning – it should be spicy and highly seasoned. Add the nuts and beat until the mixture holds together, then spread a third of it into the lined terrine.

5. Add a layer of half the ham strips interspersed with half of the chicken livers and then cover with another third of the pork mixture.

6. Add the remaining ham and livers and cover with the last of the pork mixture, before laying the final bacon slices on top, trimming the edges if necessary. Set the bay leaf on top, coverwith the lid and seal with tin foil.

7. Set the terrine in a roasting tray into which you have poured enough water to come halfway up its side. Cook in the oven for 1 hr 45 minutes to 2 hours, or until a skewer inserted for 30 seconds into the mixture is hot to the touch when taken out. The pâté should also have shrunk from the sides and the juices should be clear.

8. Cool until tepid, then remove the tin foil and lid and press the terrine with a board topped with a 900 g weight until coldKeep for two to three days before serving to allow the terrine to mature, or freeze for up to two months.

9. To serve, release the terrine from the mould, cut into thick slices and accompany with crusty sourdough bread.

Roast carrot and fennel soup

Serves 8

Ingredients

1 kg carrots, peeled, trimmed and sliced

2 bulbs of fennel, trimmed and sliced, with tops reserved to use as a garnish

1 onion, sliced

Olive oil

2 cloves of garlic, unpeeled

1.6 litres vegetable stock

100 ml single cream

Chives, chopped to garnish

Croutons to serve

Method

1. Preheat the oven to 190 C/ 375 F/ Gas Mark 5.

2. Put the carrots, fennel and onion in a roasting dish and toss with 2 tablespoons of olive oil.

3. Roast for 20 minutes, then add the garlic cloves. Stir everything thoroughly and return to the oven for 20 minutes more, until the vegetables are soft and browned.

4. Remove the papery skins from the garlic cloves, being careful not to burn your fingers!

5. Put the roasted vegetables in a large pan with the vegetable stock, bring to the boil and simmer gently for 15 minutes, then liquidise with a stick blender, until completely smooth.

6. Serve with the chopped fennel tops and chives and a few croutons.

Grace's amazing cheese scones

Makes 12

Ingredients

225 g self-raising flour

1/2 tsp salt

1 level tsp baking powder

1/2 tsp dry English mustard powder

55 g butter

140 g grated strong Cheddar cheese, plus an extra 40 g for the tops

150 ml milk

Method

1. Heat the oven to 220 ° C/425 ° F/Gas Mark 7.

2. Lightly dust a heavy baking sheet with flour.

3. Sift the flour with the salt, baking powder and mustard powder into a large bowl.

4. Lightly rub in the butter using just your fingertips, until the mixture resembles breadcrumbs. Add the cheese - not forgetting to leave 40 g for the tops.

5. Make a well in the dry mix and then carefully add the milk, mixing with a round bladed knife until it comes together into a soft, spongy dough.

6. On a lightly floured surface gently knead the dough until smooth. Roll out to a thickness of 2.5 cm and cut into the desired size and shape.

7. Gather up the trimmings and re-roll to use everything up. It is very important not to be heavy handed at this stage. Place each scone on the floured baking sheet and sprinkle carefully with the remaining cheese.

8. Bake for approximately 15–20 minutes, or until well risen and golden.

9. Leave to cool on a wire rack or eat warm from the oven with lashings of good butter.

Treacle tart

Serves 8

Rich shortcrust pastry ingredients

170 g plain flour

Pinch of salt

100 g butter

1 egg yolk

2 tbsp iced water

Filling ingredients

450 g golden syrup

Grated zest 1 lemon

2 tbsp lemon juice

1 tsp ground ginger

3 eggs, lightly beaten

115 g fresh white Breadcrumbs

Method

1. Preheat the oven to 190 C/375 F/Gas Mark 5.

2. Place the flour, salt and butter in the bowl of a food processor fitted with a steel blade.

3. Pulse gently until the mixture looks like breadcrumbs.

4. Whisk the egg yolk with the iced water; this will prevent the pastry becoming streaked with egg yolk.

5. Carefully pulse the machine whilst adding the egg mix (you may not need it all) until the mixture looks like it is starting to come together.

6. Tip onto a lightly floured work surface and gently bring together to form a smooth dough - at this point it is very important not to over work the pastry or the gluten content will make the pastry tough and heavy.

Chill for half an hour.

7. Carefully line a 20 cm tart tin with the rolled out pastry and chill once more before filling.

8. In a separate bowl, mix the syrup with the grated lemon zest and juice, then add the ginger, eggs and breadcrumbs.

9. Carefully pour the filling into the pastry case and bake for approx 30 minutes.

10. Reduce the oven temperature to 150 C/300 F/Gas Mark 2 and bake for a further 20 minutes, or until just set.

11. Serve warm with cream or custard.

Roast beef and Yorkshire puddings

Serves 10 generously

Roast beef ingredients

2.3 kg sirloin or rib of beef, (brought to room temperature)

Freshly ground black pepper

Salt

Yorkshire pudding ingredients

170 g plain flour

Pinch of salt

3 large eggs

435 ml milk

6 tbsp beef dripping or rapeseed oil

Roast beef method

1. Weigh the beef to calculate the cooking time (see below).

2. Preheat the oven to 220 ° C/425 ° F/Gas Mark 7.

3. Place the beef in a roasting tin, sprinkle with salt and pepper and roast for 20 minutes.

4. Turn the oven down to 170 ° C/325 ° F/Gas Mark 3 and roast for 20 minutes per 450 g if you like your beef medium, or 10-15 minutes per 450 g for very rare.

5. Cover loosely with foil and leave to rest in a warm place for 20-25 minutes.

Yorkshire pudding method

1. Sift the flour and salt into a bowl. Make a well in the centre and add the eggs.

2. Gently start to whisk the eggs whilst gradually adding the milk to the bowl and mix until you have a smooth batter. Chill for at least an hour before use.

3. Preheat oven to 200 ° C/400 ° F/Gas Mark 6.

4. Heat the dripping or oil in either one large tin, or four Yorkshire pudding tins, until just starting to smoke.

5. Quickly and carefully pour in the batter and, depending on the size of the pudding tin, bake for between 25-40 minutes until well risen and golden.

6. Serve immediately.

Raspberry dumplings

Serves 4

Ingredients

100 g self-raising flour

1 large pinch of salt

25 g butter

1 tbsp of granulated sugar for dumplings and another heaped dessert spoon for the raspberry sauce.

Cold milk to mix (about 4 tbsp)

300 ml water

225 g raspberries, plus a few extra to garnish

Method

1. Sift the flour and salt together in a bowl. Add the butter and rub everything in with your fingertips until it resembles fine breadcrumbs.

2. Stir in 1 tbsp of the sugar.

3. Stir in about 4 tbsp of milk and mix to form a soft dough.

4. Tear off walnut-sized pieces of dough and shape into balls. Set aside.

5. Place the water in a shallow pan and add 1 heaped dessertspoon of sugar. Gently bring to a simmer.

6. Add the raspberries.

7. Place the dumplings on top of the raspberries and place a saucepan lid on top of the pan. Simmer very gently for 25 minutes until the dumplings are nicely risen and fluffy.

8. Serve with a jug of double cream, custard or ice cream.

Vegetable pakoras

Makes 60 bite-sized pakoras or 12 large ones

Ingredients

125 g chickpea/ besan flour

25 g self-raising flour

3/4 tsp salt

1/4 tsp turmeric

1/4 tsp ground coriander

1/4 tsp ground cumin

125 ml-150 ml water

150 g potatoes, coarsely grated

150 g onions, coarsely grated

50 g fresh spinach, coarsely chopped

1/2 fresh green or red chilli, finely chopped

Sunflower or vegetable oil for frying

Method

1. Mix together both flours, the salt and all the spices in a bowl.

2. Slowly whisk in the water until the batter has the consistency of double cream.

3. Squeeze out any moisture from the potatoes and add them along with the onions, spinach and chilli. Mix well.

4. Heat the oil in a deep-fat fryer to 180 ° C/350 ° F and carefully drop teaspoons of the mixture into the hot oil.

5. Fry for 2–3 minutes until crisp and golden.

6. Drain on kitchen paper and serve immediately.

7. If you want to make bigger pakoras, use a tablespoon instead of a teaspoon to divide the mixture and fry for 4-5 minutes. Check inside one to make sure it is cooked through before serving.

8. Delicious served with a yogurt dip.

Queen of puddings

Makes 4

Ingredients

145 ml milk

145 ml single cream

15 g butter

140 g caster sugar

55 g fresh white breadcrumbs, sieved

Zest of 1 lemon

2 eggs, separated

2 tbsp raspberry jam, warmed

Method

1. Combine the milk and cream and heat gently in a saucepan.

2. Add the butter and 30 g of the sugar, stirring until the sugar dissolves, then add the breadcrumbs and lemon zest. Allow to cool.

3. Preheat the oven to 150 ° C/300 ° F/Gas Mark 2.

4. Separate the eggs, set aside the whites in a clean bowl and mix the yolks into the breadcrumb mixture. Pour into the ramekins and leave to stand for 30 minutes in the refrigerator.

5. Place the cooled ramekins into a roasting pan half-filled with hot water to create a bain-marie and bake in the oven for 15-20 minutes, or until the custard mixture is set. Remove from the oven and allow to cool slightly.

6. Increase the oven temperature to 180 ° C/350 ° F/Gas Mark 4.

7. Carefully spread the warmed raspberry jam over the top of the custard.

8. Whisk the egg whites until stiff, and then whisk in 2 teaspoons of the remaining sugar. Whisk again until very stiff and shiny and then fold in all but half a teaspoon of the remaining sugar. Pile the meringue on top of the jam-topped custard and dust the top of the meringue lightly with the last of the sugar.

9. Bake in the oven until the meringue is set and strawcoloured, which should take approximately 10 minutes.

10. Serve immediately.

Spotted dick

Serves 6-8

Ingredients

250 g self-raising flour

Pinch of salt

125 g shredded vegetable suet

180 g currants

80 g caster sugar

Finely grated zest of 2 lemons

150 ml whole milk, plus 2-3 tbsp extra

Method

1. Sift the flour and salt into a bowl and add the suet, currants, sugar and lemon zest.

2. Pour in 150 ml milk and mix to a firm but moist dough, adding extra milk if necessary.

3. Shape into a fat roll about 20 cm long.

4. Place onto a large rectangle of baking parchment.

5. Wrap loosely to allow the pudding to rise and tie the ends with string like a Christmas cracker.

6. Place a steamer over a large pan of boiling water and place the pudding in the steamer.

7. Steam for 1½ hours, checking the pan every 20 minutes or so to top up the water.

8. Remove from the steamer and allow to cool slightly before unwrapping.

9. Serve sliced with lashings of custard.

Apple and date chutney

Makes 8 x 190g jars

Ingredients

675 g cooking apples, peeled, cored and chopped

450 g small pickling onions, halved

225 g chopped dates

2 garlic cloves, peeled and chopped

1 red pepper, chopped

1 stick of cinnamon

300 ml cider vinegar

175 g soft, light brown sugar

Zest and juice of 1 orange

Method

1. Put all ingredients, except the sugar, orange zest and juice, into a large, heavy saucepan.

2. Simmer gently, stirring frequently on a low heat until the mixture is very soft and the liquid has evaporated.

3. Add the sugar, zest and juice and stir again on a low heat until the sugar has dissolved.

4. Bring to the boil and carefully stir until the mixture starts to thicken - this should take about 10 minutes. Take care as the mixture will be very hot and it can spit and splutter out of the pan.

5. Pour into sterilized, dry jars, and seal with clean, dry lids straight away.

6. The chutney will keep for a year if stored in a cool dark place.

7. It can be eaten after six weeks but, like most chutneys, the taste will improve the longer it is left to mature.

Kev's perfect bacon sandwich

Method

1. Place a heavy based frying pan on the heat and add a tiny bit of sunflower oil.

2. Add the bacon and cook until nice and crispy.

3. Remove the bacon from the pan and add a little bit more oil, and then add the egg.

4. Cook with the sunny side up.

5. Insert both the bacon and egg into a white crusty roll with a generous dollop of HP Sauce.

Serves 1

Heaven in a roll!

Ingredients

This is Kev's ideal sandwich, but you can of course use your own local ingredients!

Sunflower oil

4 rashers of thick cut, smoked back bacon (preferably from Graves of Briston, Norfolk)

1 free-range egg
(from our own hens)

1 white crusty roll

HP sauce

Nanny's lavender shortbread

Makes 50 biscuits

Ingredients

115 g unsalted butter, softened

55 g caster sugar

115 g plain flour

55 g ground rice

1 tsp fresh lavender, or ½ tsp dried lavender

Extra caster sugar for dusting

Method

1. Preheat the oven to 170 ° C/325 ° F/Gas Mark 3.

2. Beat the butter and stir in the caster sugar.

3. Sift in the flour, ground rice and lavender.

4. Work until it forms a smooth paste, wrap in cling film and refrigerate for half an hour to firm the dough.

5. Remove the dough from fridge and roll into the thickness of a pound coin.

6. Cut into your desired shape and prick with a fork before dusting with extra caster sugar.

7. Chill for approx 20 minutes until firm.

8. Bake in the oven for 15 minutes until pale golden in colour.

9. Leave to cool on a cooling rack before serving.

10. These are lovely served with summer berries and whipped cream.

We call this 'Nanny's lavender shortbread' as we use the lavender grown alongside the path leading to my parents' house.

My daughters used to call it 'Nanny's lavender', so it stuck!

Brazilian roast pork

Serves 12-16

Ingredients

6 tsp dried oregano

3 tsp cumin seeds

6 dried bay leaves, crushed

4 tsp coriander seeds, crushed

Juice of 3 limes

2 green chillies, chopped very finely

2 tbsp brown sugar

3 kg loin of pork, boned and scored

Salt

Method

1. The day before you want to cook the pork, make a spice paste with the oregano, cumin, bay leaves, coriander, lime juice, chillies and sugar.

2. Spread this mixture onto the flesh side of the pork loin, not the skin side.

3. Roll up the joint and tie with string to make a neat roll, skin side out.

4. Refrigerate for between 24 to 48 hours.

5. Remove the pork from the fridge 2 hours before you want to cook it.

6. Preheat the oven to 160 ° C/320 ° F/Gas Mark 3.

7. Rub the outside of the joint all over with salt and place in the oven for approximately two hours. Baste every 20 minutes or so with the meat juices as they start to run out.

8. If you like crackling, turn up the oven temperature to 190 ° C/375 ° F/Gas Mark 5 for the last 20 minutes or so.

9. When checked with a meat thermometer, the internal temperature should be 170 ° C/325 ° F.

10. Remove from the oven, cover loosely with foil and allow to rest for 20 minutes before carving.

Smoked trout pâté

Method

1. Put half the trout into a food processor with the horseradish, crème fraîche, sugar and lemon juice, and blend until smooth.

2. Remove from the processor, break up the remaining half of the trout into flakes, and stir in with the blended mix.

3. Mix in the herbs, paprika and pepper.

4. Spoon into a small dish and serve with slices of buttered granary or rye bread.

Serves 4

Ingredients

250 g hot-smoked trout

2 tsp horseradish root, freshly grated

1 tbsp crème fraîche

1 tsp caster sugar

1 tbsp–2 tbsp lemon juice

2 tbsp dill or chives, finely chopped

½ tsp paprika

1 tsp cracked black Pepper

This pâté formed the basis of the delicious smoked trout canapés we served at the garden party reception at Sandringham.

Kev's fried chicken

Serves 4, 2 thighs each

Ingredients

340 g plain flour

113 g dried breadcrumbs

1 tbsp salt

1 tsp ground white pepper

1 tsp garlic powder

1 tsp onion powder

1 tsp paprika

1½ tsp dried thyme

1½ tsp crushed dried rosemary

1½ tsp dried marjoram

1½ tsp dried oregano

8 chicken thighs, skinned

2 large eggs, beaten

145 ml milk

Rapeseed oil for frying

Method

1. Place all the dry ingredients in a large bowl and mix together thoroughly.

2. Wipe the chicken thighs with a paper towel and put them into the flour mix.

3. In a separate bowl whisk the eggs and milk together. Shake off any excess flour from the thighs and add them to the egg mix, two at a time.

4. Shake off any excess egg mix and then put the chickenback into the flour, carefully pressing down to get a nice thick crust.

5. Heat the fryer to 160 ° C (320 ° F) and fry the coated chicken for about 15-20 minutes. Depending on the size of your fryer you may have to do this in two batches.

6. You can check that the chicken is cooked through by cutting into a piece to have a look inside: If any of it is pink, put it back in the oil for a few more minutes.

7. Drain the cooked chicken pieces on plenty of kitchen paper and serve.

Molten chocolate puddings

Makes 12

Ingredients

350 g best dark chocolate

50 g soft, unsalted butter
(plus more for greasing)

150 g caster sugar

4 large eggs
(beaten with pinch of salt)

1 tsp vanilla extract

50 g plain flour

Method

1. You will need 12 small individual pudding moulds or ramekins, buttered.

2. Preheat the oven to 200 °C/400 °F/Gas Mark 6, putting in a baking sheet at the same time.

3. Melt the chocolate and let it cool slightly. Set aside.

4. Cream together the butter and sugar, and gradually beat in the eggs and salt, then the vanilla extract.

5. Add the flour and, when all is mixed smoothly, adin the cooled chocolate, blending it to a smooth consistency.

6. Divide the batter between the 12 moulds, put the moulds on the hot tray and place in the oven.

7. Cook for 10-12 minutes (the extra 2 minutes will be needed if the puddings are fridge-cold when you start),

8. As soon as you take them out of the oven, tip them out and serve straight away.

Dan's ham and bean soup

Serves 6-8

Soup ingredients

450g dried haricot beans (washed thoroughly and soaked overnight in cold water)

2 litres water

I cooked ham hock

4 bay leaves

225g diced carrot

225g diced celery

225g diced onion

350g shredded cooked ham

Hot sauce ingredients

50g tomato puree

2 tbsp tabasco sauce

125g butter

2tbsp white wine vinegar

1tbsp crushed garlic

4tbsp soy sauce.

6tbsp chopped parsley

Method

1. Place the ham hock in a large heavy bottomed saucepan along with the bay leaves and bring to the boil.

2. Add the carrot, celery, onions and soaked beans, cover and simmer for approx 1 hour.

3. Meanwhile in a small pan put the ingredients for the hot sauce, bring to a boil and then simmer for 10 minutes.

4. Once the ham hock has cooked, remove from the soup. Discard any fat but keep any meat and shred before adding to the shredded ham. If it seems a little thick add some water along with the homemade hot sauce and bring to a simmer for another 20 minutes.

5. Finish with the chopped parsley and serve

This is Deb's version of Dan's secret recipe.

Deb's chicken wiggle

Serves 6-8

Chicken ingredients

1.5 kg diced chicken breast or thigh fillets

40g butter

1 large diced green pepper

1 large diced red pepper

2 medium diced onions

225 g frozen peas

450g sliced mushrooms

600 ml chicken stock

600g dried egg noodles or pasta to serve

BBQ sauce ingredients

125g butter

75 ml white wine vinegar

2 tsp hot paprika

2 tsp black pepper

2 tsp salt

Method

1. In a large hot casserole dish put in 20g of butter and brown the chicken pieces. This is best done in 2 batches.

2. When they are golden brown remove them from the pan and set aside.

3. Turn the heat down slightly and into the pan add the other 20g butter red and green peppers along with the onion and cook for 5 minutes until softened. Add the sliced mushrooms and continue to cook for a further 5 minutes.

4. Put the chicken back to the pan with the vegetables, along with the chicken stock.

5. Cover and place in the oven at 180 c for 30 minutes.

6. While the chicken is in the oven, put all the ingredients for the BBQ sauce into a small pan and gently bring to a simmer. Leave to reduce slightly-about 15 minutes.

7. After the chicken has cooked for half an hour, add the peas and barbecue sauce.

8. Return to the oven for a further 15 minutes .

9. Serve with buttered noodles or pasta.

Your home recipes and notes

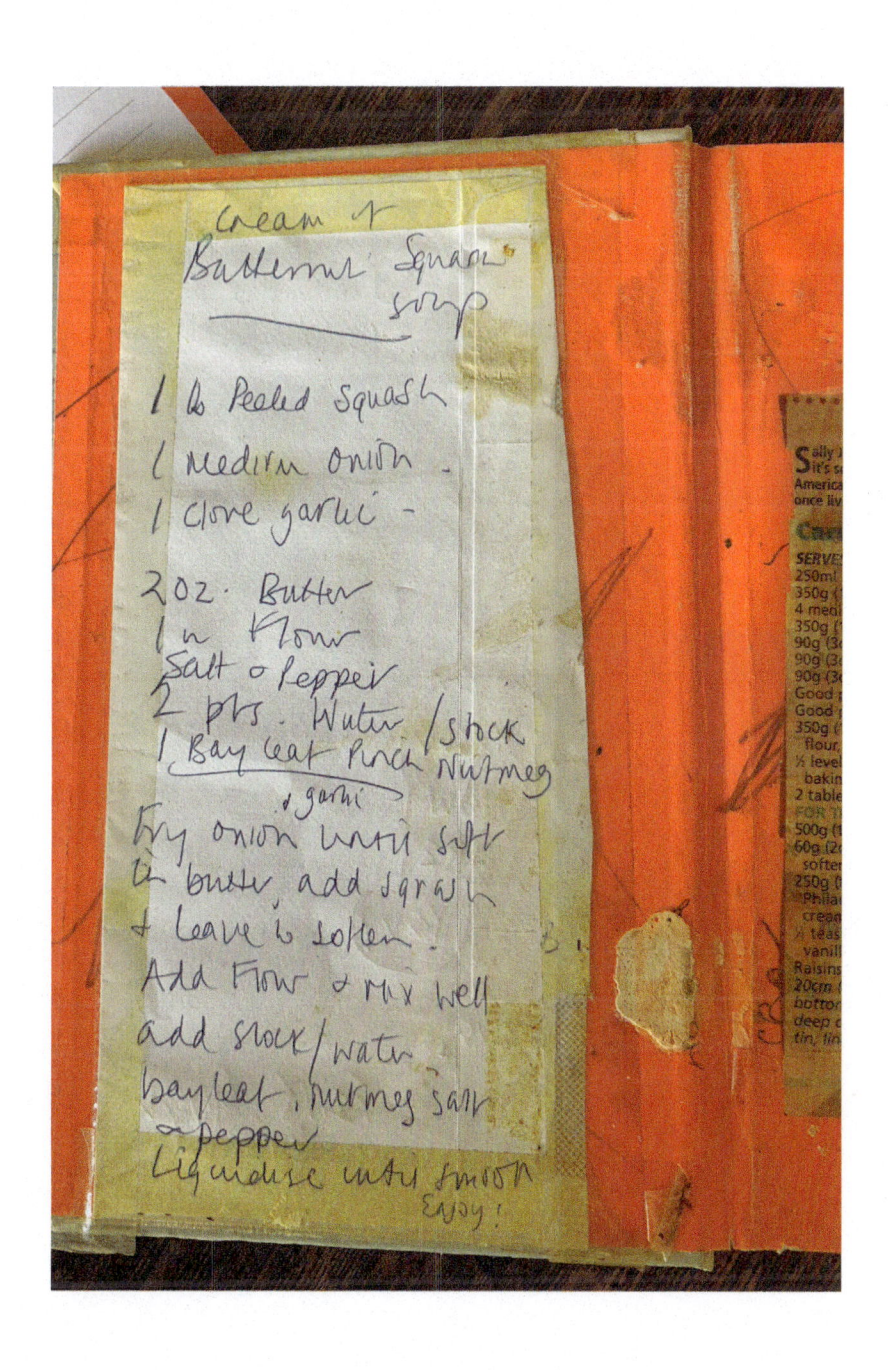

Recipe

Ingredients:

Notes:

Prep time: Serves:
Oven temp: Cooking time:

Recipe

Ingredients:

Notes:

Prep time: Serves:
Oven temp: Cooking time:

Recipe

Ingredients:

Notes:

Prep time: | Serves:
Oven temp: | Cooking time:

Recipe

Ingredients:

Notes:

Prep time: Serves:
Oven temp: Cooking time:

Recipe

Ingredients:

Notes:

Prep time: Serves:

Oven temp: Cooking time:

Recipe

Ingredients:

Notes:

Prep time:　　　　　　　　Serves:
Oven temp:　　　　　　　　Cooking time:

Recipe

Ingredients:

Notes:

Prep time: Serves:
Oven temp: Cooking time:

Recipe

Ingredients:

Notes:

Prep time: Serves:
Oven temp: Cooking time:

Recipe

Ingredients:

Notes:

Prep time: Serves:
Oven temp: Cooking time:

Recipe

Ingredients:

Notes:

Prep time:　　　　　　　　Serves:
Oven temp:　　　　　　　　Cooking time:

Recipe

Ingredients:

Notes:

Prep time: Serves:
Oven temp: Cooking time:

Recipe

Ingredients:

Notes:

Prep time: Serves:
Oven temp: Cooking time:

Recipe

Ingredients:

Notes:

Prep time: Serves:
Oven temp: Cooking time:

Recipe

Ingredients:

Notes:

Prep time:	Serves:
Oven temp:	Cooking time:

Recipe

Ingredients:

Notes:

Prep time: Serves:
Oven temp: Cooking time:

Recipe

Ingredients:

Notes:

Prep time: Serves:
Oven temp: Cooking time:

Recipe

Ingredients:

Notes:

Prep time: Serves:
Oven temp: Cooking time:

Recipe

Ingredients:

Notes:

Prep time: Serves:
Oven temp: Cooking time:

Recipe

Ingredients:

Notes:

Prep time: Serves:
Oven temp: Cooking time:

Recipe

Ingredients:

Notes:

Prep time: Serves:
Oven temp: Cooking time:

Your home recipes and notes

Sausage Rolls —
(they don't have to be perfect - just made with love)

Ingredients:
600g plain flour
2 tsp salt
125g butter ⎫ cut into small dice (1cm)
125g lard   ⎭
Cold water to mix - approx 8-10 tbsp.
1 small egg - beaten.

Dave's Sausage Rolls

Auntie Anna's

Your home recipes and notes

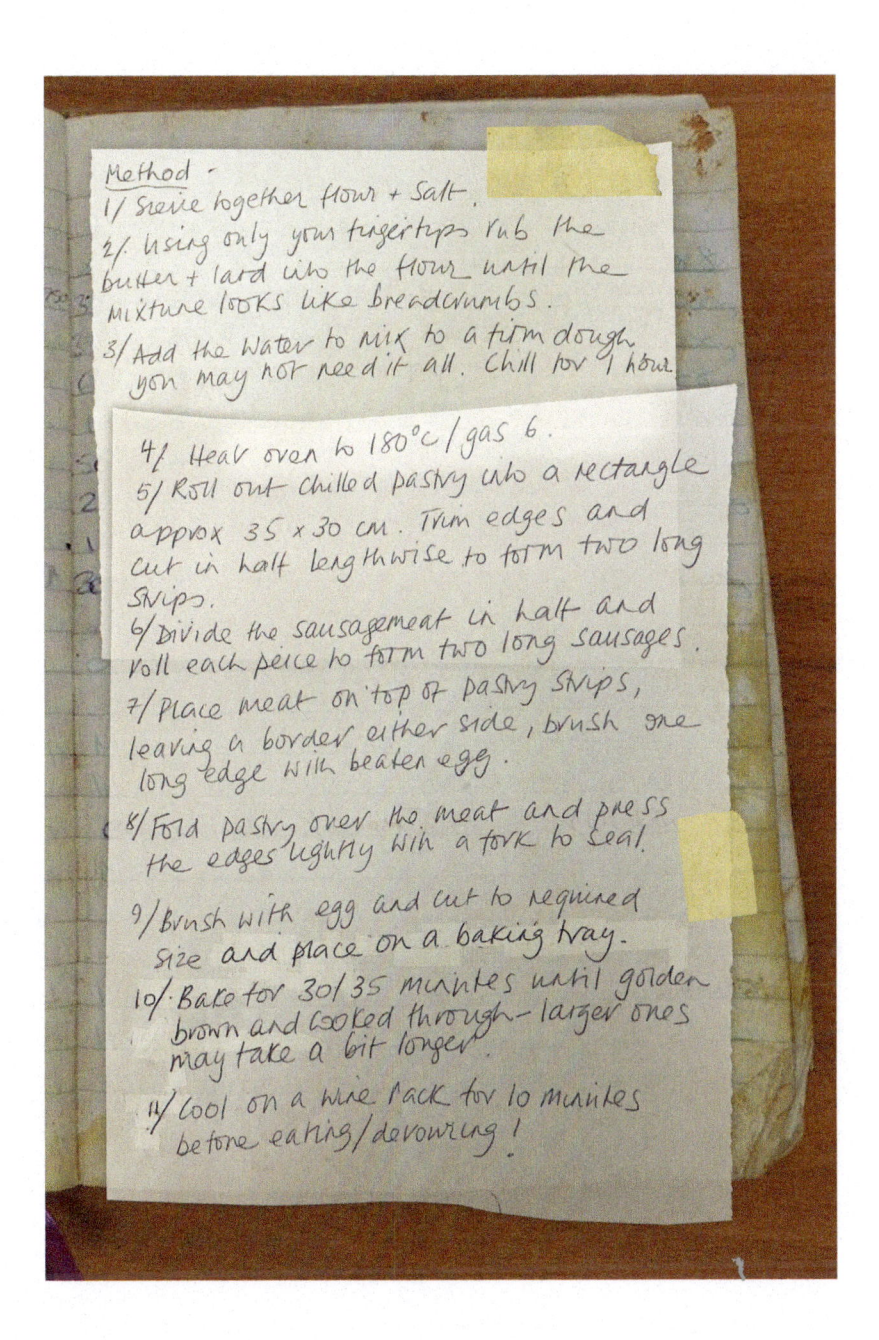

Method -
1/ Sieve together flour + salt.
2/ Using only your fingertips rub the butter + lard into the flour until the mixture looks like breadcrumbs.
3/ Add the water to mix to a firm dough you may not need it all. Chill for 1 hour.
4/ Heat oven to 180°C/gas 6.
5/ Roll out chilled pastry into a rectangle approx 35 x 30 cm. Trim edges and cut in half lengthwise to form two long strips.
6/ Divide the sausagemeat in half and roll each peice to form two long sausages.
7/ Place meat on top of pastry strips, leaving a border either side, brush one long edge with beaten egg.
8/ Fold pastry over the meat and press the edges lightly with a fork to seal.
9/ Brush with egg and cut to required size and place on a baking tray.
10/ Bake for 30/35 minutes until golden brown and cooked through - larger ones may take a bit longer.
11/ Cool on a wire rack for 10 minutes before eating/devouring!

Recipe

Ingredients:

Notes:

Prep time: Serves:
Oven temp: Cooking time:

Recipe

Ingredients:

Notes:

Prep time:　　　　　　　　Serves:
Oven temp:　　　　　　　　Cooking time:

Recipe

Ingredients:

Notes:

Prep time: | Serves:
Oven temp: | Cooking time:

Recipe

Ingredients:

Notes:

Prep time: Serves:
Oven temp: Cooking time:

Recipe

Ingredients:

Notes:

Prep time: Serves:

Oven temp: Cooking time:

Recipe

Ingredients:

Notes:

Prep time: Serves:

Oven temp: Cooking time:

Recipe

Ingredients:

Notes:

Prep time:	Serves:
Oven temp:	Cooking time:

Recipe

Ingredients:

Notes:

Prep time: Serves:
Oven temp: Cooking time:

Recipe

Ingredients:

Notes:

Prep time: Serves:
Oven temp: Cooking time:

Recipe

Ingredients:

Notes:

Prep time: Serves:
Oven temp: Cooking time:

Recipe

Ingredients:

Notes:

Prep time: Serves:

Oven temp: Cooking time:

Recipe

Ingredients:

Notes:

Prep time: Serves:
Oven temp: Cooking time:

Recipe

Ingredients:

Notes:

Prep time: Serves:
Oven temp: Cooking time:

Recipe

Ingredients:

Notes:

Prep time: Serves:
Oven temp: Cooking time:

Recipe

Ingredients:

Notes:

Prep time: Serves:
Oven temp: Cooking time:

Recipe

Ingredients:

Notes:

Prep time: Serves:
Oven temp: Cooking time:

Recipe

Ingredients:

Notes:

Prep time: Serves:
Oven temp: Cooking time:

Your home recipes and notes

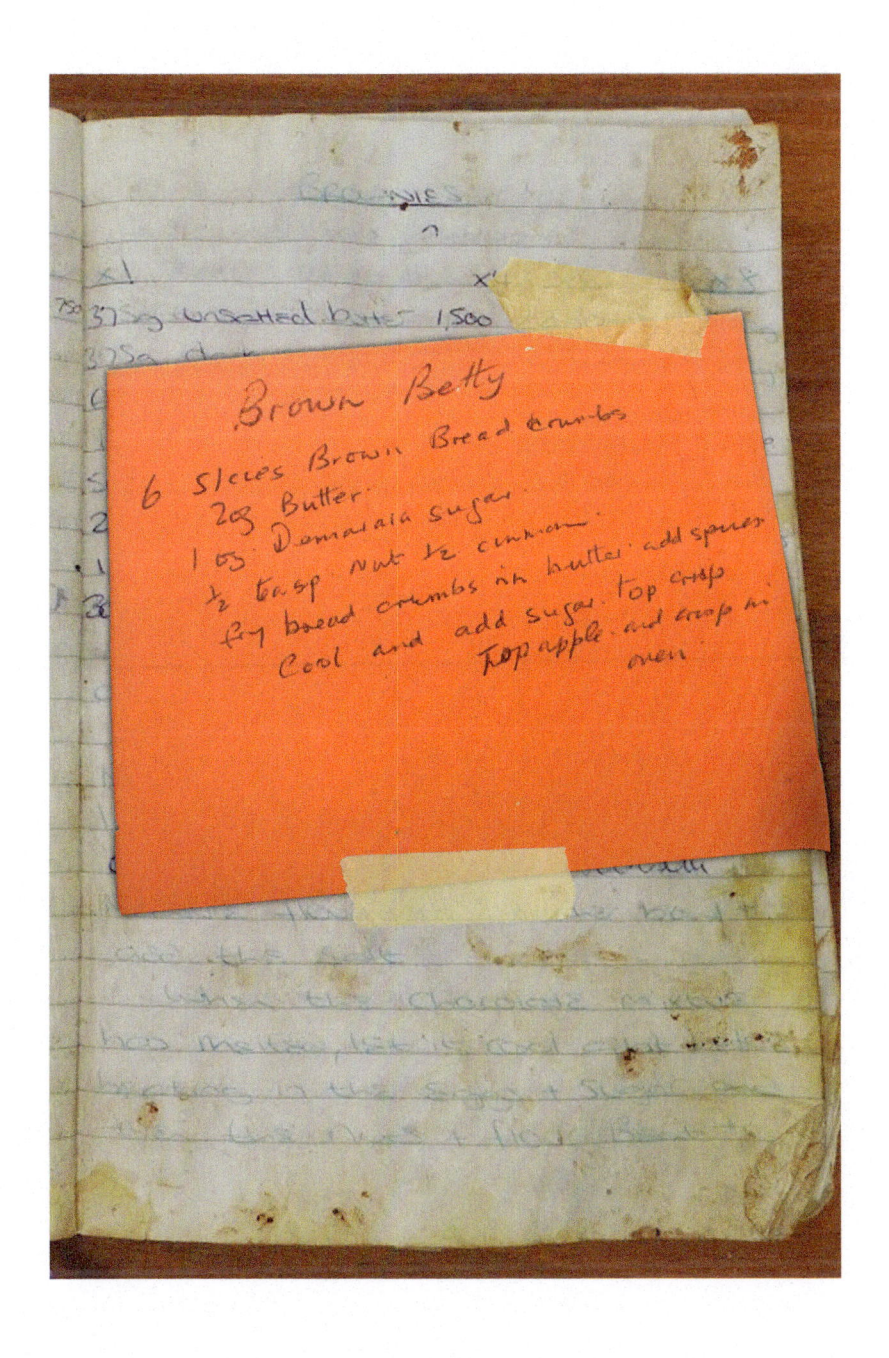

Conversion table 1

Oven temperatures

Temperature conversions

° Celsius to ° Fahrenheit ° C x 9 ÷ 5 + 32

° Fahrenheit to ° Celsius ° F – 32 x 5 ÷ 9

°C	°F	Gas Mark
140	275	1
150	300	2
170	325	3
180	350	4
190	375	5
200	400	6
220	425	7
230	450	8
240	475	9

Spoon measures

1 tablespoon = 3 teaspoons

1 level tablespoon = 15 ml

1 level teaspoon = 5 ml

1 rounded teaspoon = 2 level teaspoons

Conversion table 2

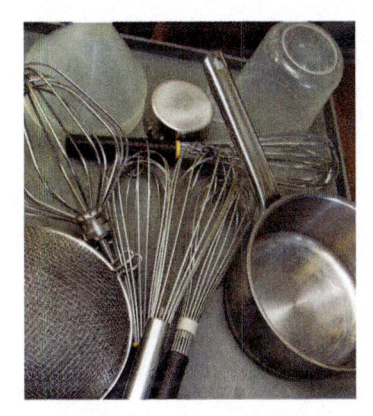

Approximate cooking equivalents

Capacity		Weight	
1/2 fl oz	12 ml	1/4 oz	10 g
1 fl oz	25 ml	1/2 oz	15 g
2 fl oz	50 ml	3/4 oz	20 g
3 fl oz	75 ml	1 oz	25 g
4 fl oz	110 ml	11/2 oz	40 g
1/4 pt	150 ml	2 oz	50 g
6 fl oz	175 ml	21/2 oz	60 g
7 fl oz	200 ml	3 oz	75 g
8 fl oz	225 ml	4 oz	125 g
9 fl oz	250 ml	5 oz	150 g
1/2 pt	300 ml	6 oz	175 g
11 fl oz	325 ml	7 oz	200 g
12 fl oz	350 ml	8 oz	225 g
13 fl oz	375 ml	9 oz	250 g
14 fl oz	400 ml	10 oz	275 g
1/4 pt	450 ml	11 oz	300 g
16 fl oz	475 ml	12 oz	350 g
17 fl oz	500 ml	13 oz	375 g
18 fl oz	550 ml	14 oz	400 g
19 fl oz	575 ml	15 oz	425 g
1 pint	600 ml	1 lb	450 g

About the author

DEBORAH STEWARD
SPECIALIST CATERING

Deborah and Kevin Steward, launched Deborah Steward Specialist Catering in 1992, a family run business, providing catering, management, consultancy and tailor made cookery courses.

Their CV includes catering for royalty and celebrities in some of Norfolk's most beautiful buildings and ensuring that countless brides and grooms have had their perfect wedding day.

SANDRINGHAM CAFÉ

Deborah and Kevin Steward began a working relationship in 2005 to manage the restaurant and cafés at the Norfolk Estate of HM The Queen. Soon after, they took over the ownership of the business.

In 2010 they were awarded the Royal Warrant as Suppliers of Event Catering and Management to HM The Queen.

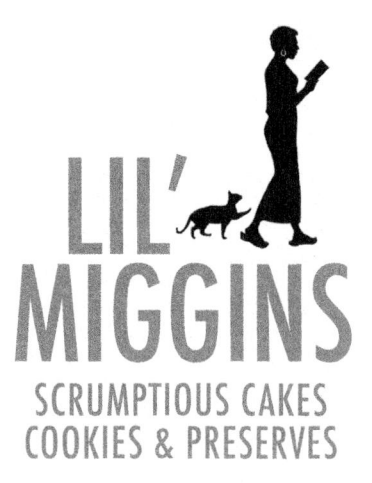

LIL' MIGGINS
SCRUMPTIOUS CAKES COOKIES & PRESERVES

For over 25 years Deborah Steward has made jam's, chutneys and relishes. Recently her Lil' Miggins range has been extended to include gluten free and vegan cakes and cookies.

All are made by hand and are available for home delivery online.

Printed in Great Britain
by Amazon